Victorian Pansies

EMBROIDERY AND PASTIMES FOR THE 21ST CENTURY

*Thank you to my wonderful parents Ron and Mary Gray,
to my sister Sue, and my three very special children - Jay, Cy and Sam
who have always been a there for me with unconditional love.
To Ezzie, my special friend, who is my soul mate and guardian of tranquility,
thank you. My gratitude and admiration to Lucie, Gloria, Marcia,
Sheila, Anna, and Cindy for exceptional talent and the gift of sharing.*

First published in 1999
by The Watermark Press & Unique Creative Opportunities,
Sydney Australia

Text Copyright © Jenny Haskins and The Watermark Press, 1999
Machine embroidery and project designs copyright © Jenny Haskins 1999
Photography copyright © Simon Blackall

Designer: Elisa Wood
Photography: Simon Blackall
Styling: Jenny Haskins
Printed and bound by South China Printing Co Ltd., Hong Kong

National Library of Australia
Cataloguing-in-Publication Data

Haskins, Jenny
Victorian Pansies : embroidery and pastimes for the 21st century
ISBN 0 949284 45 9.
1. Embroidery, Machine. 2. Flowers in art. 3. Embroidery. 4. Decoration and
ornament - Victorian style. I. Title

746.44041

Victorian Pansies

EMBROIDERY AND PASTIMES FOR THE 21ST CENTURY

Jenny Haskins

The Watermark Press

Contents

Introduction

Victoria's reign may so stamp her influence...promoting

the highest and best interests of virtue, learning, social

happiness and natural improvement of the period in which

she flourishes, that history shall speak of it as her own.

Sara Hale, editor of Godey's Lady's Book, *on the*
eve of Victoria's accession to the throne.

Society yearned for an era of grace, charm and gentility when the 'heaven sent figure of youth and innocence' in the form of Alexandrina Victoria came to the English throne in 1837.

For the next sixty-four years this slip of a girl was to guide her subjects with spiritual and moral power. Such was her influence that it reached around the globe way beyond her empire to the United States of America and even into the heartland of Europe. As Sara Hale predicted, the Victorian era was noted for its grace and charm in dress, decorations, architecture and behavior. Victoria's influence was reflected in every walk of life, but particularly in the home and family where manners and morals were key issues.

It was a gilded age where beauty and romance prospered and grew. In all things, manufactured or handmade, the inclination was to 'decorate the decorations'.

The fashions of the Victorian era reflect this abundant decoration and are recorded in postcards, books and prints as well as fabric, lace, and jewelry. Victoriana has very often proved to be addictive to those who are attracted to and love beauty and grace. Perhaps it is because these very qualities are, in some way, passed on to the beholder.

Flowers were particularly popular in the Victorian era, being portrayed in ribbon work, art work and embroidery. To me, the pansy is the consummate Victorian flower. It presents the beholder with a sweet, slightly cheeky, up-turned 'face' and its five generous frilled-edge petals have a delicate velvety sheen and texture. And then there is the color; such richness and depth and in combinations that are sometimes bold, sometimes subtle but always disarmingly beautiful.

Best of all, pansies in plant form are plentiful and can be readily enjoyed by everyone. They are equally at home in cottages and castles, on the windowsills of housing estates, in tiny urban courtyards and the spreading gardens of suburban villas.

By the time Victoria came to the throne they were the darlings of the garden bed.

My love affair with Victoriana, and in particular pansies, lured me back to painting using pansies as a subject to capture the essence of the Victorian era. Machine embroidery motifs just seemed to

Above: Marcia Pollard, a Californian colleague , made an exquisite blouse from a Vintage Victorian pattern, using my pansy design printed on silk organza, machine embroidery as well as an embroidery design taken from Marcia's new Vintage Collection disk (see credits on page 95).
Below: Cindy Losekamp of Fairfield Ohio, dedicated the pansy block (second row on left) in her silk ribbon machine embroidered pillow sampler to me. She even does beading by machine and the centers of the pansies are French knots in narrow ribbon, also sewn on the machine. I have touched on this intriguing procedure at the end of the techniques section on page 93.

follow, resulting in my Victorian Pansies machine embroidery design disk that can be used on all brands of sewing machines. This was the first of my Victorian design series trio.

Because it is exciting to see how others use the pansy designs on fabric and disk to expand and develop the original concept, I called on the expertise of well known names in the sewing and craft world. From Australia, Gloria McKinnon, renowned for her exquisite hand embroidery, Lucienne Magnay, expert sewer and editorial associate, and Sheila Pye, quilter supreme, all responded with generosity and flair. Later I found that Marcia Pollard, a colleague in California, had made an exquisite pansy print blouse from a Vintage Victorian pattern and that Cindy Losekamp of Fairfield Ohio, dedicated the pansy block in her sampler cushion to me which was a great compliment. Her glorious cushion explores the technique of silk ribbon embroidery by machine.

From the corporate world, Helmut Ott of Pfaff USA was quick to see the value of such an endeavor and was a source of support and encouragement from the outset of the project. *Victorian Pansies* is the happy result of my passion for the subject. This book is my tribute to the era; a publication full of things to make using pansies in many different forms. It's a step-by-step guide to achieving the Victorian look with a choice of fabric prints, machine embroidery, handwork, ribbon work and quilting for pictures, wall hangings, quilts, tassels, lampshades, foot stools, cushions, purses and much more.

Only natural light which captures every detail and enhances color was used in the photography in *Victorian Pansies*. All the pictures reflect directly the atmosphere and fashion that was popular in the Victorian era.

Join me now on a discovery of grace, peace and sumptuous beauty as together we venture into the world of Alexandrina Victoria who reaches out and touches the 21st century.

Jenny Haskins

General Sewing Requirements

Certain products and pieces of equipment will enhance and improve your sewing. In the materials list with each project, when general sewing requirements are included, this term refers to your sewing machine; clipping, dress making and curved-handled embroidery scissors; tape measure; pins and hand sewing needles; fabric-marking pens (air-fading and water-soluble); seam ripper and thimble. Included in the photograph are other items that regularly occur in the materials lists.

Throughout this book I have graded each project according to its relative simplicity/complexity.

 easy   medium   advanced

If you are a beginner don't be discouraged from attempting something that is advanced. You learn as you go, develop skills and, if necessary, become adept at disguise. A whispy bow or a piece of lace will hide a less than perfect seam or hem. Take liberties with the projects, rearranging decorative elements and changing them entirely to suit your needs and what you have close at hand in your work basket.

1 Pfaff 7570 embroidery/sewing machine
2 Scissors for cutting and clipping
3 Self-adhesive tear-away fabric stabilizer
4 Jenny Haskins Victorian Pansies and Victorian Scrolls and Curlicues design disks
5 Rayon 40 embroidery threads
6 Hand painted lace
7 Wired ribbon
8 Silk ribbon for hand embroidery
9 Hand embroidery threads
10 Hand embroidery needles
11 Gold metallic thread
12 Pfaff Jenny Haskins

Choice card
13 Fabric-marking pen; air-fading on one end, water-soluble on the other
14 Quilting ruler
15 Rotary cutter and self-healing mat
16 Seed beads
17 Jenny Haskins Victorian satin print
18 Machine embroidered pansy
19 Pellon H640/fusible batting (wadding)
20 Vliesofix/Wonderunder (iron-on fusible web)
21 Antique dyed rayon lace
22 Tape measure

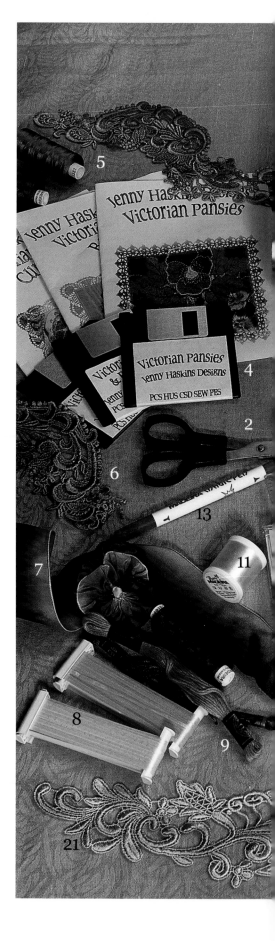

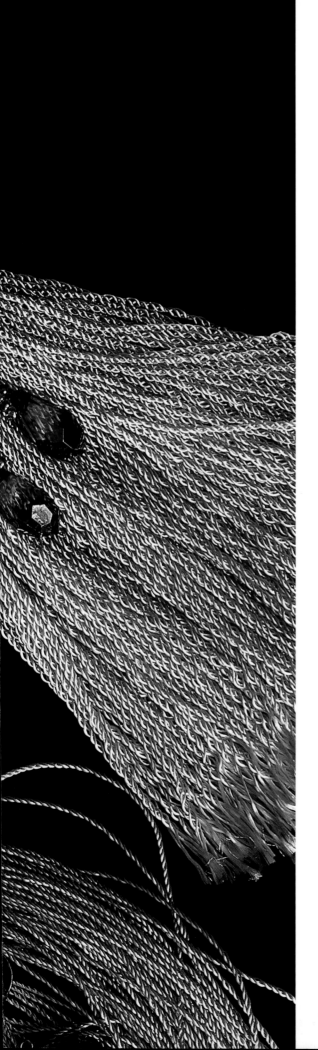

Silken Strands
Pansy Tassels

❧

Who can resist fondling the silken strands of a tassel? These lavish-looking accessories that were particularly in vogue during the 19th and early 20th centuries have double appeal because they look lovely and feel good too.

Whether used as a key handhold, on a curtain tie back, attached to a pull cord for a light or to add a distinctive finishing touch to a garment, fashion accessory or some element of home décor, a tassel always commands attention.

This simple adaptation of a tassel with a pansy as its head is a perfect example of achieving a maximum effect with a minimum of effort and skill. The project uses the Victorian Pansy design disk and requires a domestic sewing machine software program to access the design and download it to a blank memory card to stitch out the motif.

MATERIALS

- 20cm (8in) square of off white nylon organza
- 20cm (8in) square of melt-away heat dissolving stabilizer
- 1 reel each of Rayon 40 embroidery thread: purple, grey/lilac, soft yellow
- Victorian Pansy design disk formatted for all machine brands
- Blank memory card
- PC-design software
- 1 pre-wound bobbin
- 30cm X 300mm(12in x 12in) wide rayon fringing, antique dyed (see page 82)
- 10cm (4in) of drop beading attached to a ribbon header
- 5cm (2in) gold edging braid
- 12.5cm (5in) hand painted rayon lace drop (see page 83)
- 1 tube of 450 craft glue or clear flexible craft glue
- Small piece of batting
- 40cm (16in) narrow gold cord
- 1 card of bias tape to bind the inner embroidery hoop
- Small pair of scissors
- General sewing requirements

1 Use the bias tape to bind the inner hoop, finishing the end with a small hand stitch or glue. See photograph 1.

2 Gather together the melt-away stabilizer and the nylon organza and the bound and unbound sections of the hoop. See photograph 2.

3 Assemble the hoop with nylon organza on top and stabilizer beneath with the rough side of the stabilizer facing up. See photograph 3.

✂ TIP ✂ Binding the inner hoop gives more tension when stretching fine fabrics in the hoop and helps hold them very taut thus ensuring accurate stitching.

1. Bind the inner hoop
with bias tape

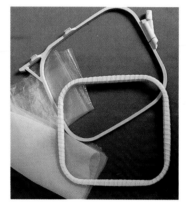

2. Hoop sections,
stabilizer and organza

3. Assemble the hoop,
organza on top

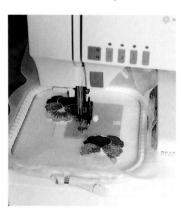

4. Download and stitch
out pansies

5. Cut out each pansy,
iron from wrong side

6. Apply glue to
fringe top

4 Download Pansy1 from Victorian Pansies on to a blank design card. Stitch out two pansies using the threads from the materials list that best match those used. The second pansy should be mirrored. See photograph 4.

5 Remove the stabilizer and fabric from the hoop and carefully cut out each pansy close to the edge of the stitching, then iron each motif with a hot steam iron from the wrong side. See photograph 5.

6 Antique dye the fringing (see page 82), dipping the bottom edge of the fringe into the more concentrated solution. When the fringe is dry, lay it flat and place glue on the flat braid section at the top of the fringe. See photograph 6.

7 Roll glued braid section of fringe into a very tight cylinder. See photograph 7.

8 Use some threads from the fringe to wrap and tie the fringe to form a tassel head with a 'waist' below. See photograph 8.

9 Layer the lace next to the tie, then the beading and the gold braid positioning to suit. See photograph 9.

10 Glue in place following the above order. See photograph 10.

11 Lay one pansy face down on a flat surface, then position a small piece of batting in the upper section of the pansy along with the knotted ends of the narrow gold cord (folded in half to form a loop). See photograph 11.

12 Glue in place before gluing the tassel head between the top and bottom-embroidered pansies and glue together around the edges. Pin until the glue is partially dry, then remove pins. Do not use tassel for 24 hours.

7. Roll-up glued fringe
top tightly

8. Tie a 'waist' with
self threads

9. Layer lace, beading
and gold braid

10. Glue layered
trims in place

11. Position cord and batting between the two pansy motifs
and glue in place before incorporating the tassel.

Shades of Light
Victorian Lampshade

Take a very inexpensive lampshade and in a matter of minutes you can turn it into a designer/decorator item that will become the focal point in a room. Using lace motifs, a silk print, wonderful fringing lace and a butterfly brooch, the plainest lampshade is transformed into an eye-catching object d'art. There's no sewing involved; dye the lace and fringing first, let them dry and then glue all the trims in place.

MATERIALS

- *1 purchased cream lampshade, top diameter 10cm (4in) bottom diameter 28cm (11in)*
- *1 small Victorian silk print (medium 1003)*
- *2 lace motifs antique dyed (see page 82)*
- *91.5cm x 130mm (1yd x 5in) fringing lace (dyed as above)*
- *1 small butterfly clip*
- *1 tube of 450 craft glue or clear flexible craft glue*
- *General sewing requirements*

TIP Make sure the join of the lampshade is at center back of the shade and that the fringing lace starts and finishes at this point. The print should be positioned opposite this point.

1 Use a water-soluble fabric marking pen to mark the center front of the lampshade.

2 Cut the silk print into an oval shape that fits between the top and bottom edges of the shade.

3 Glue the fringed edging lace to the bottom edge of the lampshade overlapping the beginning by 2.5cm (1in).

4 Place glue on the outside edges of the print then place it on the centre front of the lampshade. Press it firmly with the fingers making sure the print lies flat without bubbles.

5 Snip the lace motifs into pieces that will surround and frame the print in an attractive way. Place glue on the back of lace segments, then position them over the raw fabric edge of the print.

Choose a suitable base to show off your new shade to its best advantage.

Victorian Footstool
and Pincushion

More decorative than practical, these footstools and pincushions are a delightful means of displaying silk prints, laces, beadwork, embroidery and fringing. They capture the essence of the Victorian era and will dress up any room. The pincushions held beautiful hatpins while the footstools were for a dainty slippered foot. You may choose to make either or both as elaborate or plain as you please.

MATERIALS

✄ NOTE ✄ You will need half the materials to make the pincushion in width and length.

✄ *25cm (10in) diameter foot stool or 12.5cm (5in) diameter pincushion*

✄ *36cm (14in) bias cut silk print or square (foot stool large 1003, 1008 small repeated and 1055 large) or 18cm (7in) bias cut silk print or fabric square (pincushion small 1055)*

✄ *1-2 hand dyed or painted lace motifs (see page 82)*

✄ *75cm x 25mm (29 1/2in x 1in) gold edging braid or fringing*

✄ *1 pkt small glass antique beads*

✄ *Beading needle and thread*

✄ *Hand embroidery needle*

✄ *Machine or hand embroidery threads in your choice of colors*

✄ *Vliesofix/Wonderunder*

✄ *1 tube 450 craft glue or clear flexible craft glue*

✄ *Staple gun (upholstery model)*

✄ *Phillips head screw driver*

✄ *Tin of stain/varnish*

✄ *Small paint brush*

✄ *General sewing requirements*

✄ NOTE ✄ You can enhance the print with either hand embroidery or machine embroidery or leave it plain. I used a small lace butterfly from my signature disk by Cactus Punch or you may choose to use the small butterfly and lace motif from my Pfaff Choice card. Beading and rows of machine or hand embroidery can enhance the flowers and outline the hearts.

1 Use the Phillips head screwdriver to remove the screw from the wooden base to separate the padded top from the wooden base. Then use the stain/varnish and brush to paint the wooden base of the stool/pincushion and set aside to dry. You may need to apply two coats. See photograph 1.

2 You may choose to use either machine or hand embroidery to quilt, outline and enhance the silk print. Stitch No 01 (top stitch length 1.5) can be used to quilt cross hatch lines before beading, stitch No 60 (width and length 6.0, density 0.25) can be used to outline the hearts or use a small applique stitch outlined with stitch No 154. The cheeks and beard of the pansies can be accented with a freehand long stitch anchored at each end with a tiny straight stitch.

3 A machine-embroidered or lace butterfly, or some other motif can also be placed either over the heart or between the hearts.

1. Separate top from base (above) and apply varnish to base.
2. Stitch a bead in each corner of the intersecting lines (opposite).

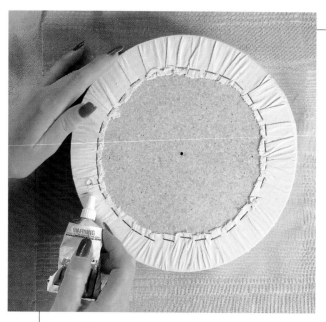

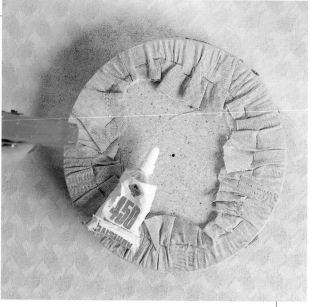

3. Apply glue to the underside of top.

4. Staple the fabric into position.

4 Beading is sewn after the hand or machine embroidery is completed. You may choose to bead the intersecting lines or the outside edge of the heart or create clusters of beads. See photograph 2.

5 When you are happy with your beading and embroidery, press with a steam iron from the wrong side over a towel.

6 Center the embroidered print over the padded top of the stool and pin in the center.

7 Turn the padded top upside down, on a flat clean surface, then run the glue around the outside edge of its underside, extending

2.5cm (1in) in to the center - allow to set slightly. See photograph 3.

8 Pull the print fabric in around the edge of the stool until it is very tight and the top and sides have no wrinkles. The bias cut of the fabric assists this process; persevere until the fabric is completely smooth as the end result is worth the effort. If desired, staple the fabric to the underside of the top with a staple gun. See photograph 4.

9 Cut away excess fabric from the underside of the stool top and remove the pin from the center front of the print.

5. Cut lace in pieces at connecting bars.

6. Steam press web-backed lace into position.

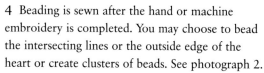

7. Spread glue on upper surface of base.

8. Re-join top and base with center screw.

10 Apply Vliesofix/Wonderunder to the back of lace motifs (see page 84) and cut the lace motifs into several pieces cutting only where connecting bars separate the lace segments.
Then trim away the remains of the connecting bars. See photograph 5.

11 Position these lace pieces, right sides up, to overlap the embroidered print, then fix them in place by pressing them with a steam iron. See photograph 6.

12 Spread glue on the upper face of the base. See photograph 7.

13 Re-join the top and wooden base with the center screw. See photograph 8.

14 Using glue, trim the edge of the stool where the top and base meet with gold edging lace or braid to cover the join. You may choose to use two different braids/trims with one sitting over the other. See photograph 9.

15 You may choose to add an ornate antique button, or some butterfly motifs to the stool/pincushion top to give that truly Victorian look.
Beaded hatpins can be placed in the pincushion to add character and age to the project.

9. Glue and trim edge with fringed braid.

10. The finished stool.

Pansy
Sewing Case

Reminiscent of a Victorian lady's sewing parlor, this sewing case is beautiful, practical, and will make a romantic addition to your sewing basket. A fabric print graces the front, there are machine embroidered pansies on the back and six embroidered pansy faces form flaps and pockets inside for storing sewing essentials.

MATERIALS

- 24cm x 28cm (9¹/₂in x 11in) moiré grosgrain
- 1 moiré grosgrain pansy heart print 1008 large
- 60cm x 112cm (24in x 45in) light to mid toned colored silk dupion (to be antique dyed)
- 1.6m (1³/₄yd) fine piping to match silk dupion
- 15cm x 90cm (6in x 36in) Vliesofix/Wonderunder
- 20cm x 50cm (8in x 20in) iron-on tear-away stabilizer
- 30cm x 50cm (12in x 19³/₄in) Pellon H640/fusible batting
- 25cm x 50cm (10in x 20in) woven iron-on interfacing
- 50cm (20in) self-adhesive tear-away stabilizer
- 3m x 25mm (3¹/₄yd x 1in) cream or white edging lace (to be antique dyed)
- I rayon lace motif
- 2.5cm x 70cm (1in x 27¹/₂in) gold organza ribbon for ties
- 2.5m x 6mm (¹/₂yd x ¹/₄in) dark olive silk ribbon for embroidery
- Tapestry needle for ribbon embroidery
- Small piece of cream fabric for the pins and needles inserts
- Packet of seed beads in variegated colors to match shades of print
- Beading needle and thread
- Rayon 40 machine embroidery threads 1 reel each of: dusky purple, gold, gray, olive green and dark green
- Metallic thread, 1 reel gold
- Monofilament thread, 1 reel
- Construction thread, 1 reel to match fabric
- Rayon hand embroidery thread: dark olive, dusky purple and lemon/gold for French knots
- Hand embroidery needle
- Pre-wound bobbins or fine bobbin thread
- Machine needles: size 80 embroidery needle and size 90 metallic needle
- Machine feet: open-toe embroidery foot, clear-view freehand/darning foot and zipper foot
- Tracing paper
- 30cm x 50cm (12in x 19³/₄in) heavyweight cardboard
- Victorian Pansies disk formatted for all brands of sewing machine
- PC-design software
- Blank memory card
- Pfaff Creative Fantasy card No 28
- Fine tipped paintbrush
- HB pencil
- Pinking shears
- General sewing requirements

PREPARATION

1 Use the antique dyeing technique on page 82 to dye the silk dupion, the narrow edging lace and the lace motif. The silk used was a gunmetal gray and this rich color is the result, so experiment.

2 From the dyed silk fabric cut 6cm (2¹/₄in) strips across the width of the fabric joined to measure two 1.5m (60in) lengths.

3 Cut a 30cm (12in) strip across the width of the silk fabric. To obtain the crinkled effect in the silk, twist the wet silk into a rope, secure with elastic bands on either end to hold in place until the fabric is dry. When the fabric is dry unravel the twists and lay the fabric flat on an ironing board, place a similar sized piece of woven interfacing over the crinkled fabric and fuse the interfacing to the back of the crinkled dyed silk.

✂ TIP ✂ 1cm (³/₈in) seam allowance was used throughout this project.

4 Iron Pellon/fusible batting to the back of the pansy print and the grosgrain fabric then use the HB

pencil and tracing paper to trace the pansy print heart shape. Transfer the heart shape to the card and cut out two heart shapes with the cutting line 3mm (1/8in) outside the drawn line. Put to one side.

5 Use the water-soluble pen to trace the one heart shape onto the center of the grosgrain fabric; this will become the back. Trace two heart shapes onto the crinkled silk fabric adding seam allowances.

QUILTING

6 Lower the feed dogs, use monofilament thread, the clear-view freehand embroidery foot and a straight stitch to outline quilt the pansies, leaves and buds on the front pansy print.

EMBROIDERY

✁ TIP ✁ Use the self-adhesive tear-away , size 80/90 embroidery needle, rayon 40 embroidery thread and a pre-wound bobbin for all embroidery. Refer to page 86 in the techniques section for the use of the self-adhesive tear-away.

7 Use the PC-designer software to transfer 'pansy1', 'bud2' and 'leaf2' to a blank memory card.

Single Pansy Embroidery

8 Use the remaining dyed silk fabric to embroider six pansies using gold and dusky purple rayon embroidery thread with metallic gold centers and outlines. Allow at least 5cm (2in) between each pansy and 10cm (4in) of fabric below two of the pansies which will be cut out in a 'cone' shape for the scissors and tape-measure pockets.

Back Embroidery

✁ TIP ✁ Either print or stitch a template for the pansy, bud and leaves to ensure perfect embroidery placement.

9 Use the photo as a guide to thread colors and placement to embroider the back heart section. Embroidery is within the heart shape and done in the following order:
—at the top right and bottom left, embroider design No 7 from card No 28 using olive green, gray and dusky purple rayon embroidery thread
—trace around buds, leaves and pansy then embroider 'bud2' in dusky purple and olive green over lower section of top right embroidery No 7
—over the bud stem embroider a pair of 'leaf2' using olive green and darker green rayon embroidery threads
—use the same colors to embroider 'leaf2' mirror image overlapping the bottom design No 7
—'bud2' mirror image is embroidered over the base of top 'leaf2' using same colors as first bud
—'pansy1' is embroidered over the bud stem and leaves using dusky purple and gold rayon threads with a metallic gold thread outline.

10 Remove excess stabilizer from back of all embroidery; press and pull the fabric into shape. Moisten all the embroidery with water. Refer to the techniques section on page 82 to mix a darker mixture of potassium permanganate in a small plastic bowl then use the fine paintbrush and a minute amount of the dye to carefully shade the pansy, buds and leaves to give an antique effect. Remove any water-soluble pen lines and allow to dry. Press gently.

11 Place the pansy cone shape, from the pattern sheet, over the two pansies that have an extra fabric margin, matching the pattern pansy to the embroidered one. Trace the shape then cut along outer cutting line.

Cut out the remaining four pansies allowing a 1cm (^{3}/8in) fabric border for turning.

INSIDE SEWING CASE

12 Clip fabric along edges and around top of pansy embroidery on the two cone shapes and the four single pansies then turn to the back and press flat.

13 Iron Vliesofix/Wonderunder to a piece of dyed silk, large enough to fit the four single pansies and the pansy cones. Use the HB pencil to trace around the four single and two cone pansy fabric shapes on the paper side of the Vliesofix/Wonderunder and cut out. Peel the paper from the back of the fabric, position and press onto the reverse sides of the pansies and cones covering the turned-back edges.

14 Cut two pieces of cream fabric with pinking shears to fit under needles and pins pansies.

Positioning the inside pansies

15 Using the photo as a guide, center a pansy cone pocket on each inside heart fabric piece with the point at the heart point and a single pansy in each top curve of the heart, and pin.

Pansy flaps

16 Insert the two pieces of cream fabric under the two middle pansies (flaps) then pin through the top of the pansies. Use monofilament thread, open-toe foot and a small pin-stitch to stitch around the top of the pansies, catching the fabric inserts.

Pansy pockets

17 The outer single pansies and the pansy cones are pockets. Use monofilament thread and a pin-stitch to sew the pansies and pansy cones in place starting and finishing on either side of the gold petals to form pockets.

HAND EMBROIDERY

18 Thread the tapestry needle with the green silk ribbon and use a ribbon stitch (see page 92) to embroider leaves in and around the pansies on the print and the embroidered back.

19 Thread the hand embroidery needle with several strands of hand embroidery thread to embroider groups of French knots (page 92) in yellow, purple and green thread amongst printed and embroidered pansies and leaves. Use gold metallic thread to embroidery centers of both printed pansies.

20 Use the seed beads, a beading needle and thread to bead the embroidered and printed lattice on the front and back heart pieces.

ASSEMBLY

21 Check the back heart outline against the front heart shape and draw a line on the back that matches the stitch line on the printed front heart. Cut out both hearts adding seam allowance.

22 With raw edges aligned and using the zipper foot, sew the piping to the seam line of each heart overlapping the ends. Attach the narrow edging lace in the same manner with the scallops pointing towards the center of the hearts, starting and finishing at the point of the heart.

23 Join the ends of each of the frill pieces to form a circle then press all seams open. Fold the frill in half lengthwise and press. Gather each frill to fit around the heart and pin in place over the lace and the piping, aligning the raw edges and stitch in place.

24 Cut the organza ribbon in half, pleat one end of each piece and pin, aligning the raw edges of the pleated ribbon with the raw fabric edges using the photo as a guide to positioning, then sew in place.

25 Like making a cushion, sandwich the frill, lace and piping between the front and one of the 'crinkle' hearts, with right sides together. Sew around the seam line leaving an opening in the side without the ribbon large enough for turning and to insert the card heart. Repeat for the remaining hearts. Clip seams and turn, then insert the card into each heart and slipstitch the opening closed. Topstitch with matching thread close to the piping using the zipper foot and needle positions.

26 Cut a piece of the silk 2.5cm x 15cm (1in x 6in). Seam down the long side and across one short side, turn to right side, turn in the raw ends and slipstitch closed. Press flat with the seam on the edge. This piece becomes the hinge. Position the hinge fabric on the side opposite the ribbon on each heart piece and hand stitch in place close to the edge of the heart beneath the frill from the front and over the crinkled fabric on the inside of the sewing case. Position the coffee colored lace motif over the center of the 'hinge' on the inside and hand sew in place. To complete, insert scissors and tape in the long pockets, thread and buttons in the small pockets and pins and needles in the flaps.

Hanging Heart Delight

Brooch/Stickpin Cushions

Beautiful to look at, delightful to hold - these hearts can be used as brooch cushions, filled with lavender and hung in a window, or used as pure decoration hanging from a handle or mirror knob. You may choose to make one or two with either cream or black lace trims.

MATERIALS

To make one heart cushion

- 1 heart silk print (large 1007, 1008 OR 1009)
- 1 fabric piece to match the size, shape and shade of the heart print fabric
- Iron-on Pellon H640/batting to fit the back and front fabric pieces to make the cushion
- 72cm (28¹/2in) insertion piping cord in black and gold OR cream
- 1.04m (41in) either black (4in) (wide) OR cream 5cm (2in) (narrow) edging lace
- .5m x 25mm (¹/2yd x 1in) old purple shaded wired ribbon for pansy
- 15cm x 25mm (6in x 1in) 3 old green shaded wired ribbon for leaves
- 1 pkt of assorted antique glass beads
- Beading needle and thread
- 1 pkt of fine wire (to fit through beads)
- 1 tassel (either purchased or made)
- 50cm (20in) Marcia Pollard's heavy duty soluble stabilizer
- 1 reel of construction thread to match lace
- Rayon 40 embroidery threads 1 reel each of: warm brown green, dark black purple, golden yellow, brown/green and cream
- 1 reel of monofilament transparent thread
- 35cm (14in) narrow velvet ribbon for hanging
- Criswell Romantic lace designs disk
- PC-design software
- Pfaff Mothers Day card No. 15
- Blank memory card
- 50cm (20in) self-adhesive tear-away
- Machine needles: size 80/90 large eyed needle and size 60 sharp needle
- Machine feet: open-toe embroidery foot, zipper foot and clear-view freehand embroidery foot
- Hand sewing needle
- Small amount of Toyfill
- General sewing requirements

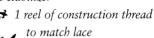

PREPARATION

1 Iron the Pellon/fusible batting to the back of the heart print and backing fabric.

2 Rule a diagonal grid across the backing fabric using a water fading fabric pen with lines 2.5 (1in) apart.

TECHNIQUES

3 Use the open-toe embroidery foot and size 80/90 large-eyed needle to sew either the hand quilting stitch No 11 or a top stitch No 01 to quilt the diagonal grid lines on the heart backing fabric using cream or dark purple thread.

4 Use the PC-design software to download Pansy spray from the Victorian Pansy design disk, and lace designs of your choice from the Criswell lace design disk onto a blank memory card.

5 Using the self-adhesive tear-away stabilizer in the hoop as shown in the techniques section on page 86, embroider a pansy spray from card No. 15 over the quilted grid on the heart backing fabric with the embroidery threads in the materials list.

6 Place one layer of Marcia Pollard's heavy duty soluble stabilizer in the hoop, stretched drum tight, to embroider three small hearts in warm brown/green and two lace scrolls in cream from the Criswell lace collection.

7 When completed, roughly cut around the

embroidered lace designs then rinse in hot water to remove the soluble stabilizer. Dry flat before pressing.

8 Freehand outline quilt the pansies, leaves and buds on the silk heart print using the clear-view freehand embroidery foot, monofilament thread in a size 60 needle and a straight stitch with the feed dogs dropped or lowered.

9 Position either the little Criswell lace hearts or scrolls at the top and/or bottom of the heart and sew in place using the freehand technique described in step No 8.

10 Press the front and back heart pieces with a steam iron, gently pulling them into shape, then cut the pieces out to match allowing 2cm (3/4in) for seams.

11 Use the zipper foot, matching construction thread and correct needle positions to sew the insertion braid to the outside edge of the silk heart print fabric.

12 Slightly gather up the lace to fit the outside edge of the heart, starting and finishing at the point of the heart. Leave the width of the lace in length as an overlap on each end of the lace to make a sharp miter to join the lace. Pin, then sew the lace to the silk heart print with the straight side of the lace and the raw fabric edges of the heart aligned. Join the lace with a sharp miter.

✂ TIP ✂ Arrange more gathers on the curves to allow the lace to sit flat.

13 Fold the narrow velvet ribbon in half lengthwise and lap the ends over the lace to form a loop with the raw edges of the ribbon, lace and fabric aligned in the center of the heart dip at the top of the heart. Bunch up the scalloped lace edges and flatten them by pinning towards the center of the front to reduce bulk.

14 Place the cushion back over the cushion front with right sides together.

15 Use the zipper foot, construction thread and needle positions to sew the cushion front to the cushion back leaving a 10cm (4in) opening in one side for turning being careful not to catch the scalloped edge of the lace in the seam.

16 Clip seams before turning to the right side to remove the pins and pull up the ribbon hanger. Fill the heart shape with Toyfill making sure that the rounded top and sharp point of the heart are tightly filled with stuffing.

17 Hand sew the opening closed in the side of the cushion.

18 Refer to page 92 to make the ribbon pansy and leaves; the center will be beaded instead of knotted.

19 Refer to page 16 to make a pansy tassel or purchase a tassel.

20 Stitch beads to the center of the ribbon pansy. Looped strings of beads can also be attached from behind to hang down from the bottom of the pansy. The fine wire can have beads threaded onto it, then made into loops, which can be attached behind the pansy. Attach the three leaves behind the pansy.

21 Attach the tassel to the bottom of the heart using either hand sewing or glue.

22 The pansy can be attached to the top or bottom of the heart as you choose.

23 Stick pins or brooches can now be pinned to the heart to add character and age.

The Heart of a Pansy

❧❧

Luscious antique wired ribbon pansies with clusters of silk ribbon embroidered flowers cover a pansy heart print, illustrating the extravagance of Victorian decorations. The saying 'there is never too much' seems appropriate for this embellished heart cushion.

MATERIALS

🐇 1 Victorian Pansy silk print No 1007 or 1008 large, front of heart

🐇 30cm (12in) matching silk fabric for heart backing

🐇 30cm (12in) Pellon H640/fusible batting to back silk print

🐇 2m x 10cm (2^1/4yd x 4in) antique cream edging lace

🐇 75cm (29^1/2in) gold insertion cord

🐇 1 roll of fine cord for tassel in black gold colors

🐇 1 hank of 4mm (^{1}/8in) Thread Gatherer silk ribbon, color Egyptian Nights or 4-5m x 4mm (4-5yd x ^{1}/8in) variegated silk ribbon in shades of pink-purple for hand embroidered silk flowers

🐇 1m x 4mm (1^1/8yd x ^{1}/8in) old gold silk ribbon for silk ribbon embroidery flower centers

🐇 1.5m x 25mm (1^5/8yd x 1in) wired purple ribbon for pansies

🐇 50cm x 25mm (20in x 1in) Hanna silk, wired green ribbon for leaves

🐇 50cm x 7mm (20in x ^{1}/4in) old gold silk ribbon for wired pansy centers

🐇 Small piece of buckram to back wired pansies

🐇 Old gold embroidery thread

🐇 Green hand embroidery thread

🐇 Size 13 chenille embroidery needle

🐇 Size 24 tapestry needle

🐇 1 small black lace motif

🐇 Toyfill

🐇 General sewing requirements

PREPARATION

1 Iron the Pellon/fusible batting to the back of the silk heart print.

2 From the matching silk fabric cut a heart shape to match that of the silk print outline, adding a 1cm (^{3}/8in)-seam allowance.

RIBBON EMBROIDERY, WIRED TASSELS AND LEAVES

3 Refer to page 92 in the techniques section and use the purple wired ribbon and buckram to make two pansies. The 25mm (1in) silk ribbon is used for the pansy centers.

4 Refer to page 94 in the techniques section and use the green wired ribbon to make four pansy leaves.

5 Trim the buckram from the back of the pansies and stitch two pansies with the leaves behind them, on the silk panel to compliment the printed pansies.

6 Use the Egyptian Nights silk ribbon and the size 24 tapestry needle to embroider clusters of small ribbon stitch flowers, with five petals, in and around the embroidered and printed pansies. The center of each flower is a French knot made from the 7mm (^{9}/32 in) old gold silk ribbon. Refer to page 92 for stitches.

7 Use the chenille needle and three strands of green thread to embroider leaves around the flowers using lazy daisy stitch. Refer to page 92.

8 Use one strand of old gold embroidery thread and the chenille needle to straight stitch over the lattice with a small French knot on each cross bar.

TO MAKE THE TASSEL

9 Refer to Four Beauties on a Fan on page 53 for directions to make a tassel from fine cord. The tassel has a lace motif overlaid with the third ribbon pansy (hand stitched in place) covering the tassel wrap and tie, adding a unique finish.

CONSTRUCTION

10 Complete the heart cushion using the gold insertion cord and wide edging lace as for steps 12 to 17, page 35. Add tassel to the heart tip to cover the join in the cord.

11 A Victorian dress clip is the finishing touch.

Cluster of
Cushions

ᴀ·ᴀ

Sometimes the simplest ideas are the most charming and appealing. These magic little cushions started out as silk prints which were filled with lavender and tied together with silk organza ribbon.

MATERIALS
- *3 medium Victorian prints No 1003 (antique fabric)*
- *25cm (10in) soft lavender organza*
- *Lavender or potpourri to fill the cushions*
- *2m (2¹/4yd) narrow gold piping cord or insertion braid*
- *1 reel of construction thread*
- *1.5m x 25mm (1²/3yd x 1in) gold organza ribbon*
- *Size 75 universal needle*
- *Zipper foot*
- *General sewing requirements*

METHOD
1 Leave a 2cm (³/4in) seam allowance around the imprint lines on the silk print then cut each one out
2 Cut the soft lavender organza to match the above – cut three.
3 Use the construction thread, size 75 universal needle and the zipper foot to sew the piping around each cushion along the imprint line on the silk print.
4 Place the organza square over the silk print, with right sides together and pin in place. Stitch around all sides, leaving an opening for turning on one side.
5 Cut away excess fabric from the seams and turn cushion to the right side.
6 Fill the cushion with lavender then hand-sew the opening closed.
7 Repeat for all three cushions.
8 Place the cushions one on top of the other and tie as if a parcel with a bow at the top. You may choose to place a bunch of pansies to the top of the stack for added interest.

Pansies are Purple

Romantic fabrics, hand dyed laces and trims combined with spectacular machine embroidery make this cushion a unique work of art. This is a great project to use those short ends of lace as the trim around the inner border of the cushion is asymmetrical.

MATERIALS

- 1.5m (1^2/3yd) lilac silk fabric cushion back and top
- 20cm (8in) floral contrasting fabric for inner border
- 60cm (^{2}/3yd) Pellon H640/fusible batting
- 12.5cm (5in) Vliesofix/Wonderunder
- 3m x 115mm (3^3/8yd x 4^1/2in) wide edging lace (outside edge of cushion lace A)
- 70cm x 50mm (27^1/2in x 2in) scalloped white edging lace (two inner edges of cushion lace B)
- 70cm x 25mm (27^1/2in x 1in) border lace to be antique dyed, see page 000 (two inner edges of the cushion lace C)
- 70cm x 75mm (27^1/2in x 3in) edging lace to be antique dyed, see page 82 (opposite inner edges of the cushion lace D)
- 1 tin/pkt purple Dylon or Rit cold water dye
- Rayon embroidery threads one reel of each: dark black/purple, soft gray/mauve, soft golden/yellow, white, metallic gold, warm brown/green and dark brown/green
- 1 reel construction thread
- Pre-wound bobbins
- Machine needles: size 80/90 large eyed needle and size 75 universal needle
- Machine feet: open-toe embroidery foot, clear-view freehand embroidery foot
- Victorian Pansies and Victorian Scrolls and Curlicues design disks formatted for all machine brands
  - PC-design software
  - 1 blank memory card
    - 50cm (20in) self-adhesive tear-away stabilizer
    - Cushion insert
  - General sewing requirements

PREPARATION

1 From the lilac silk fabric cut a 56cm (22in) square for the cushion front and a rectangle 76cm x 56cm (30in x 22in) for the cushion back.

2 From the Pellon fusible batting cut one 56cm (22in) square.

3 Iron the Vliesofix/Wonderunder to the back of the floral border fabric.

4 From the floral inner border fabric cut two 6cm (2^3/8in) strips across the width of the fabric.

5 Cut the above into four equal lengths.

6 Using the mitering technique on page 89, in the techniques section, join the fabric strips to make a square with mitered corners with the outside edges measuring 42cm (16^1/2in). Place to one side.

7 Follow the manufacturers instructions and use the purple cold water dye to dye the wide edging lace A and the narrow scalloped lace B. You may need to mix a little black with the dye to 'age' the color.

8 Follow the directions on page 82 in the techniques section, to antique dye the remaining lace.

9 Transfer the embroidery placement diagram from the pattern sheet to the center front of the cushion top using a water-fading pen.

EMBROIDERY

10 Follow the directions found on page 86 in the techniques section, use self-adhesive tear-away in the embroidery hoop for stabilizing the fabric for embroidery.

11 Using the PC-design software and the Victorian Pansies down load pansy No 1, pansy bud No 1, fronds, and set of leaves to a blank memory card. From Victorian Scrolls and Curlicues down load the ribbon swag.

✂ TIP ✄ The embroidery is numbered on the

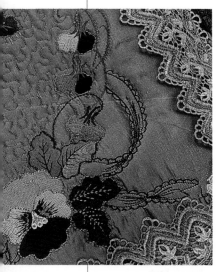

Ribbon swag

Pansies and leaves

Stipple quilting

pattern sheet in sequence so follow the numbers in order to get the desired effects of layering.

12 Using the black purple thread and a size 80/90 large eyed needle and a pre-wound bobbin, embroider the ribbon swags. You will need to manually embroider the ribbon tails if you wish, using a small straight stitch edged with a narrow scallop using photocopy paper at the back as stabilizer.

14 Embroider the pansy buds, fronds, flowers and leaves in sequence using threads from the materials list that best match those used. Refer to the picture.

15 When the embroidery is complete, remove any excess stabilizer from the back of the embroidery and remove all the pen lines with a clean damp cloth.

16 Place a towel on the ironing board, then place the embroidered cushion top face down over the towel and press with a hot steam iron from the wrong side of the fabric, stretching the fabric as you go.

17 Iron the Pellon/fusible batting to the back of the cushion top.

18 Place the clear-view embroidery foot on the machine and thread with pale mauve thread (to match the fabric) and outline-quilt all the embroidery using a freehand straight stitch.

19 Freehand stipple-quilt

the plain fabric area within the embroidery design.

20 Lay the mitered corner inner border fabric centered over the cushion top and the embroidery design and then iron it to the cushion top. This border will sit within the edges of the cushion top.

✂ TIP ✂ Stitch all lace down on both edges to hold flat, using the open-toe foot and size 75 universal needle.

21 Stitch the narrow purple edging lace B around two sides of the cushion top aligning the edge of the lace with the inside edge of the border fabric, with the scallops facing out.

22 Stitch the gold edging lace D to the other two sides of the cushion top with the straight side of the lace parallel to and 1.5cm (1/2in) from the outside edge of the border fabric. The scalloped edge of the lace should face to the center of the cushion and cover the raw fabric edge of the border fabric. Miter the corner of the lace and cut the other two edges of the lace at an angle of 45 degrees. Then cover these edges and the mitered corner with small lace medallions.

23 Place the narrow border lace C over the purple scalloped lace so it covers the raw fabric edges of the border fabric.

24 Cut the cushion backing fabric in half so each piece measures 38cm x 56cm (15in x 22in) and use your preferred overlap method to make up the cushion, making buttonholes (if desired) before attaching the front to the overlapped back. Turn through to the right side of the cushion and press.

25 Attach the wide purple edging lace to the outside edge of the fabric border aligning the straight edge of the lace with and over the raw fabric edge and mitering the corners. Stitch though all layers back and front of cushion when attaching the lace.

✂ TIP ✂ To prevent the lace from 'flopping' forward, use a freehand stipple stitch and thread to match lace to anchor it to the edge of the cushion.

26 Place the insert in the cushion and place it on your favorite Victorian sofa.

Fascinating Fan Wall Hanging

Fans have always fascinated me and this rich and luxurious wall hanging 'grew' from my silk paintings of pansy fan segments; the originals have now been reproduced as silk prints. The same techniques could be employed to create a framed picture, a cushion top, the center block of a quilt or as a feature panel on a garment.

MATERIALS

- 56cm (22in) green/gold silk dupion with a grid of pin tucks (fabric was purchased with pin tucking already stitched – if you are working with fabric without pin tucks and want to sew them, allow sufficient extra fabric for this)
- 76cm (30in) black/purple self patterned backing and binding fabric
- 5 silk print fan segments No 2000
- 56cm (22in) Pellon H640/fusible batting
- 50cm (20in) Vliesofix/Wonderunder
- 50cm (20in) self-adhesive tear-away stabilizer
- 50cm (20in) Marcia Pollard's heavy duty soluble stabilizer
- 50cm x 25mm (20in x 1in) black/purple silk organza ribbon
- 50cm x 20mm (20in x ^{3}/$_4$in) olive green silk organza ribbon
- 6 lace medallions best matched to those used [you may need to antique dye these (see page 000) to age the lace]
- Rayon 40 embroidery threads, one reel each of: black/purple, gray/mauve, olive green and yellow/gold thread
- 1 reel of construction and monofilament thread
- Pre-wound bobbins
- Criswell Romantic lace design disk formatted for all machine brands
- PC-design software
- Blank memory card
- Photocopy paper for stabilizer
- Pfaff Fantasy card No 15, pansy design and card No 1, small violet spray
- Size 80/90 large eyed machine needle
- Machine feet: open-toe embroidery foot and clear-view freehand embroidery foot
- General sewing requirements

PREPARATION

1 From the green/gold pin tucked silk dupion and the Pellon/fusible batting cut out a 56cm (22in) square.

2 Iron the Pellon/fusible batting to the back of the pin tucked fabric.

3 Use the pattern from the pattern sheet and the fabric-marking pen to transfer the fan design onto the above fabric, centering the design.

4 Iron Pellon/fusible batting to the back of the fan segment prints and then iron Vliesofix/Wonderunder to the back of the Pellon/fusible batting. Cut the fan segments out remembering to cut around the pansies and leaves accurately at the top of each segment.

EMBROIDERY

5 Using the PC-design software download the 'fleurish' design from Criswells Romantic lace disk, to a blank memory card.

6 Place two layers of Marcia Pollard's heavy-duty soluble-stabilizer in the embroidery hoop making sure it is drum tight.

7 Using the black/purple embroidery thread in the bobbin and the needle and a size 80/90 large eyed needle embroider nine 'fleurish' designs.

8 When embroidery is complete, roughly cut around the designs then immerse in hot water to remove the stabilizer and lie flat to dry, before ironing from the wrong side of the embroidery.

9 Use the self-adhesive tear-away stabilizer technique found on page 86 to embroider the small violet spray in the center of each fan segment, just below the printed pansy using threads of your choice from the materials list.

10 Use the technique on page 84 to iron the Vliesofix/Wonderunder to the back of the embroidery and lace medallion pieces. Put these pieces to one side.

11 Use the layout on the pattern sheet to lay out then pin the lace and fan segments in place. The lace sits under the pansies at the top of the fan, under the sides of the fan and under and over the base of the fan to add interest.

✂ TIP ✂ Make sure the fan segments overlap each other as a fan does and the center segment is centered in the fan shaped outline on the wall hanging.

12 Iron all pieces in place using a hot steam iron.

13 Lower the feed dogs and use the clear-view freehand embroidery foot, monofilament thread and a narrow zigzag to sew down all the raw edges of the fan segments, around the cut fabric edges of the pansies and leaves and the outside edge of all lace pieces.

14 Freehand outline-quilt the pansies and leaves using a straight stitch.

✂ TIP ✂ Use photocopy paper as a backing stabilizer for built-in stitching embroidery.

15 Use the black/purple embroidery thread pre-wound bobbin, size 80/90 embroidery needle and the open-toe embroidery foot to appliqué over the raw fabric edges of the fan print.

16 Sew rows of built-in embroidery stitches in the following order:
—stitch No 188 down the inside edge of the fan segments on either outside edge of the fan
—stitch No 60 (width and length 6.0, density 0.25) down each fan segment with the scallops all facing the one way
—stitch No 165 (width and length 4.0, density 0.25) on the raw edges of the outside fan segments
—stitch No 57 (width 6.0, length 10.0, density 0.25) on the outside edge of the previous row of embroidery
—stitch No 60 (width and length 6.0, density 0.25) mirrored over the curved bottom edge of the fan.

17 Use the layout on the pattern sheet, matching thread colors to those used in the photo, to embroider the pansy design from card No 15 on either side of the fan.

18 Iron the 'fleurish' embroidery motifs in place (see photo). Then lower the feed dogs and use the monofilament thread, the clear-view freehand embroidery foot and a straight stitch to sew right around the outside edge of the embroidery motifs.

19 Press the embroidered fabric, layer it over wrong side of the black/purple backing fabric then cut out the drawn fan outline.

20 Pin the backing fabric to the quilt top, then using construction thread sew all layers together close to the raw edges of the fabric

21 Cut 10cm (4in) wide bias strips from the dark purple fabric, joined together to measure 72cm (28$\frac{1}{2}$in) in length. Cut another strip the same width 23cm (9in) in length.

22 Follow the bias binding technique on page 90 for the sides and top of the wall hanging, pleating the binding to follow the curves on the top of the wall hanging.

23 Join the bottom bias strip using the straight technique for the top and bottom of a quilt on page 91 to complete the quilt binding.

24 Lower the feed dogs, use the clear-view freehand embroidery foot, matching thread in the bobbin to the quilt backing and monofilament thread in the needle to straight stitch outline quilt between the fan segments, around the fan, lace and embroidery motifs to complete the quilt.

You may choose to pin a butterfly brooch to the top of the fan. An antique dress clip holds the organza ribbons (olive green and black/purple) laid over each other and tied in a bow at the base of the fan for that typically Victorian over-the-top touch.

Four Beauties
on a Fan

The fan shape is frequently used as a repeated block in quilt making, but here it is greatly enlarged to become a single decorative element for displaying four fabric print portraits of a Victorian beauty. You can have fun with the jewelry and embellishments, ringing the changes on each of the prints if you wish. The color choice is important in order to obtain that lavish, rich Victorian feeling. Purple, green/gold and cream set the mood but you could just as successfully work with blues, green or gold as long as the tones, patterns and textures look and feel right.

MATERIALS

- 1.5m x 115cm (1²/₃yd x 45in) dark purple polyester jacquard fabric
- 1m x 115cm (1¹/₈yd x 45in) dark purple polyester satin
- 50cm x 115cm (20in x 45in) green/gold printed polyester jacquard fabric
- Remnants of cream lace fabric
- 60cm x 115cm (²/₃yd x 45in) cream silk dupion (to be antique dyed, see page 82)
- 2m x 94cm (2¹/₄yd x 37in) Pellon H640/ fusible batting
- 2m x 90cm (2¹/₄yd x 36in) Vliesofix/Wonderunder
- 50cm (¹/₂yd) self-adhesive, tear-away stabilizer
- 1m (1¹/₈yd) tear-away stabilizer
- 5m x 15mm (5¹/₂yd x ⁵/₈in) rayon edging lace with a deep scallop (to be antique dyed, see page 82.)
- 4m x 10mm (4¹/₂yd x 3/8in) dark olive green braid
- 4 Victorian Lady silk prints, large No 1014
- 4-5 rayon lace motifs hand painted in colors to match prints (see page 83)
- 2 or 3 medium sized cream rayon lace motifs for the fan handle
- 3 teardrop crystal beads
- Pfaff Richelieu and Appliqué card No 7
- 1 reel fine cord in dusky purple for the cord and tassels
- Rayon 40 embroidery thread: one reel each of: ivory, deep cream, deep olive and dusky purple
- 1 reel metallic gold embroidery thread
- 1 reel Monofilament thread
- Bobbinfil or two pre-wound bobbins.
- 4 reels dark purple construction thread
- Machine feet: open-toe embroidery foot, clear-view freehand embroidery/darning foot, quarter-inch foot
- Machine needles: size 90 embroidery needle and size 90 Metafil needle
- Hand sewing needle
- Teflon mat
- Black cotton sewing tape
- Pencil and ruler
- General sewing requirements

FINISHED QUILT/WALL HANGING SIZE
approx. 96cm x 102cm (37³/₄in x 40¹/₂in)

PREPARATION
1 Use the method on page 82 to antique dye the lace and silk dupion to match the silk prints.
2 Using the oval pattern from the pattern sheet centered over the silk prints, lightly mark the oval shape using the water-soluble fabric-marking pen.

CUTTING
3 From the dark purple jacquard fabric cut:
—one, 90cm x 95cm (35¹/₂in x 37¹/₂in) rectangle for the quilt
—four 9cm (3¹/₂in) wide strips across the width of the fabric for the binding.
From the green/gold printed jacquard fabric cut:
—four 4cm (1⁵/₈in) strips the length of the fabric for the borders.
From Pellon/fusible batting cut:
—one 90cm x 95cm (35¹/₂in x 37¹/₂in) rectangle and fuse to the back of the dark purple polyester

jacquard fabric rectangle

—two 4cm (1^5/8in) strips the length of the fusible batting for the borders then cut in half and fuse to the back of the green/gold border fabric strips.

—four ovals as per the pattern sheet then fuse to the back of the prints, centering them in the drawn ovals. From Vliesofix/Wonderunder cut:

—four 2.5cm (1in) strips the width of the fusible web for the binding.

PREPARING FABRICS FOR APPLIQUE

Note: Fan frame is cut from silk dupion, the silk print frame from the green/gold fabric, small and large wedge shapes from the lace remnant fabric.

4 Use the patterns from the pattern sheet and the pencil to trace four outlines each of the above patterns (except the small wedge) on the paper side of the Vliesofix/Wonderunder. Draw three outlines of small wedge. Cut around these slightly larger than drawn.

5 Iron the above shapes to the wrong side of the appropriate fabrics, centering the ovals over the Pellon/fusible batting on the back of the prints.

6 Use the technique on page 84 to apply Vliesofix/Wonderunder to wrong side of lace motifs.

EMBROIDERY

Print

7 Lower the feed dogs, then use the freehand embroidery foot, monofilament thread and a straight stitch to outline-quilt the pansies, leaves and the lady.

Note: Use tear-away stabilizer under the built-in stitches used for embroidery.

8 Refer to the photo as a guide to embroider the

jewelry in the following order:

—pearls and pearl earrings embroidered in ivory rayon 40 embroidery thread, using stitch No 165, length and width 3.0, density 0.25

—gold chain embroidered in metallic gold thread using stitch No 11, Length 2.0

—pendant and drop earrings embroidered in dusky purple rayon embroidery thread, single pattern stitch No 65, length 6.0, width 3.0, and density 0.25. with a single pattern of stitch No 11 in metallic gold thread above the embroidered diamond.

✂ TIP ✂ Assemble the fan one segment at a time commencing with the left fan segment which sits under the next segment for a fan layering effect.

9 Remove the paper backing from the cut out pattern pieces for one complete fan segment: fan frame from silk dupion, oval frame from green/gold fabric, oval of lady print and large lace wedge.

10 Position the cream silk dupion fan frame on the dark purple fabric and pin in place then insert the large lace wedge shape behind the lower frame 'window' and pin in place. See diagram 1 on pattern sheet.

Position the print in the center of the oval 'window' and pin. The green/gold inner frame is positioned over the print and under the silk dupion. Make sure an even amount of green gold fabric is showing around the print.

Position the straight side of the rayon edging lace under the outer edge of the frame as in diagram 1. Carefully remove pins while pressing all pieces in place.

Embroidered appliqué

11 Appliqué the fan segment, attach the lace and seal the raw edges of all fabric pieces in the fan using the open-toe foot, size 80 needle, pre-wound bobbin and tear-away stabilizer by embroidering:

—around the outside and inner wedge edges of the silk dupion fan frame using stitch No 62 length 7.0, width 3.5 and density 0.25 using deep cream rayon embroidery thread

—around the outer edge of the green/ gold oval frame using stitch No 62 , length 7.0, width 3.5 and density 0.25 in deep olive embroidery thread. On the outside of this row of stitching sew another row using the same thread and stitch No 51, reduce width and length to suit curve.

— around the inner edge of the green/gold fabric frame using stitch No 165 length and width 4.0 and density 0.25 using dusky purple embroidery thread. Then on the outside of this row of stitching sew another row using the same thread and stitch No 52 width and length 6.0 and density 0.25

12 To position the small lace wedge, lay the second segment frame in place sitting over the right side of the first frame. Position the small lace wedge between the segments where they meet and pin. See diagram 2 on the pattern sheet. Remove the second fan segment frame to position the straight edge of the scalloped edging lace under the upper curved edge of the lace wedge and press in place using the Teflon mat.

13 Pin the straight edge of the scalloped edging lace from the first segment that overlaps the lace wedge back, out of the way, to use a small zigzag stitch and attach the lace fabric by sewing down the two edges that border the fan. Attach the edging lace while appliquéing the curved edge of the small wedge, as on the first segment, using the oval stitch and deep cream rayon thread. Remove pins.

14 Repeat for remaining three fan segments and two wedges.

Embroidery motifs

Note: Refer to page 86 for the self-adhesive tear-away stabilizer technique.

15 Use card No 7, bow design to embroider and appliqué a bow in each of the large lace segments. Iron Vliesofix/Wonderunder to the back of one of the cream silk dupion ovals (made by cutting the fan segment out) for the automatic appliqué built into the embroidered bow design.

Note: Refer to page 83 for painted lace technique.

16 Apply Vliesofix/Wonderunder to the back of the painted lace motifs (refer to this technique on page 84) then remove the backing paper and cut into smaller sections to position on the small and large fan wedge shapes referring to the photo as a guide. Press in place using the Teflon mat. Place and attach the two cream lace motifs for the fan handle in the same manner.

PUTTING IT TOGETHER

17 Using the quarter-inch seam foot, attach the top and bottom border strips to the quilt. Trim away excess fabric from the end of the strips, then attach the side borders. Trim ends.

18 Attach the quilt top to the satin backing fabric using the quilting through with Audrey's Bond Powder technique on page 88.

19 Lower the feed dogs and use the clear-view freehand embroidery foot, thread to match the fabric in the needle and bobbin, and a straight stitch to stipple-quilt the background of the quilt top.

20 Attach the lace motifs with monofilament thread and freehand straight stitching around the edges.

21 Trim the backing fabric to match the quilt top and attach the quilt binding using the straight quilt binding technique in the techniques section on page 91.

22 Position and pin the olive green braid in place along the inner edge of the borders folding under the raw ends. Stitch in place using monofilament or matching thread, open-toe foot and a zigzag stitch.

ATTACHING HANGER LOOPS

You may choose to make four loops for hanging from the remaining fabric.

Cut a piece of dark purple fabric 11cm x 90cm (4 1/2 in x 35 1/2 in). Fold in half lengthwise with right sides together and sew along the long edge using a narrow seam to make a tube. Turn to the right side and press with the seam positioned at the center back. A narrow strip of the green/gold fabric could be sewn down the middle lengthwise for extra trim. Cut into four equal lengths and pin to the top of the quilt with equal distance apart. Turn under the raw edges and sew in place by hand.

CORD

Cut two, 3m (3 3/8 yd) lengths of narrow cord, stabilize them by knotting them around a door knob then twist both together from the other end until they start to curl around one another. With one hand, hold the twisted cord in the middle to fold the cord in half and hold the ends with the other hand. Allow the strands to twist together evenly thus making a cord. Release from doorknob, smoothing the twists with your hand to make them even, and then knot the ends.

TASSEL

Cut a 25cm (6in) length of black tape. Place the end of the tape under the presser foot of the sewing machine. Then sew slowly while looping the narrow cord over the tape with the right hand side of the loop extending just past the tape and the left-hand side of the loop a little longer than the length you want the tassel. See diagram 3 on pattern sheet. Cut the sewn tape in half to make two tassels.

Lay one length of looped tape flat then lay one end of the twisted cord over the tape with the knot just extending beyond the tape. Roll up the tape firmly then hold in place by stitching by hand. Lift the cord up and the strands of cord will fall back and cover the tape. Wind a length of cord around the head of the tassel and tie to hold it in place.

Thread the ends of the tie to the middle. Repeat for the other tassel.

Tie in a double bow and then hand sew to the base of the fan.

Hand sew the crystal beads to the lower edge of the lace motifs on the three small lace wedges.

Captivating Pansies

❧❧

Silk prints stand on their own and can be framed just as they are, accented as with the previous project or used as a design basis for embroidery. Here I have used the printed image in a similar way as one does a needlepoint canvas, but the sewing machine does most of the work.

MATERIALS

- Pansy silk print No 1004 (large) on cream fabric
- 41cm (16in) square of Pellon/fusible batting
- 1.22m x 50mm (1¹/₃yd x 2in) scalloped edging lace
- 2 lace motifs to be antique dyed (see page 82)
- 4 narrow lace corner motifs to be antique dyed (see page 82)
- Rayon 40 embroidery threads one reel each of: golden yellow, black/purple, black/green, warm brown/green, gray/mauve, cream and white
- Pre-wound bobbins
- Victorian Pansies design disk formatted for all machines
- PC-design software
- Blank memory card
- Pfaff Jenny Haskins Choice card
- 50cm (20in) self-adhesive tear-away
- 50cm (20in) Vliesofix/Wonderunder
- 3 sheets of photocopy paper to act as stabilizer
- Size 80/90 large eyed needle
- Machine feet: open-toe foot and clear-view freehand embroidery foot
- 3 pkts of antique glass seed beads in green luster, purple luster and pink pearl
- 9 seed pearls
- Beading needle and thread
- Silk ribbon for embroidery in gray/mauve and gray/green
- Tapestry needle to suit the above
- General sewing requirements

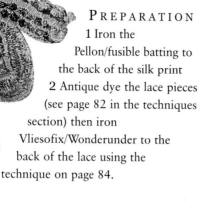

PREPARATION

1 Iron the Pellon/fusible batting to the back of the silk print

2 Antique dye the lace pieces (see page 82 in the techniques section) then iron Vliesofix/Wonderunder to the back of the lace using the technique on page 84.

EMBROIDERY

Built-in Stitches

3 Use a pre-wound bobbin, size-80/90 large eyed needle, open-toe embroidery foot, warm brown/green thread and photocopy paper as stabilizer at the back of the print to embroider:

—stitch No 01, length 1.5 over the cross hatch lines in the center of the heart and the heart outline

—stitch No 165 (width and length 4.0, density 0.25) stepped out in a memory to form a double row of stitching around the outside edge of the heart and around the top of the top fan shape

—stitch No 60 (width and length 6.0 density 0.25) around the inside of the heart shape, with the scallops pointing to the center

—stitch No 147 width 4.0 length normal around the top arch of the fan shape close to stitch No 165 following the curve

—stitch No 146 with 4.0 length normal over the fan 'ribs' following the curve, repeating the rows until the fan shape is covered.

Change to gray/mauve thread to sew:

—stitch No 165 (width and length 3.0, density 0.25) following the outside edge of the ribbon tails and loops.

FREEHAND EMBROIDERY

4 Lower the feed dogs to use the clear-view freehand embroidery foot and black/green thread to outline the pansy leaves and veins.

5 Use cream thread to stipple-quilt the imprint area around pansy print.

Motif Embroidery

6 Use the Victorian Pansy disk and the PC-design software to download Pansy No 1 to the blank memory card.

7 Use the self-adhesive tear-away stabilizer technique on page 86 to embroider three pansies over the pansies on the print, matching the directions of the printed pansies.

8 Use the thread colors from the materials list and photo as a color placement guide.

✂ TIP ✂ Stitch the pansies by moving the color on manually rather than automatically. Press the pattern start button or the foot control to find where the pansy starts, then position the printed pansy under the needle so the needle sits where the bottom petal starts on the right hand side. (You may need to test sew this to understand it more clearly.) The outline for the bottom petal should roughly follow that of the printed pansy. If it does not, then stop the stitching, unpick the stitches and reposition the print under the needle.

9 Use the Jenny Haskins Choice card to stitch a small butterfly in warm brown/green thread in the top right corner, just above the print, using the photo as a guide to position.

COMPLETING THE PICTURE

10 Iron the scalloped edging lace around the imprint lines on the silk print to measure approximately 20cm x 25.5cm (8in x 10in) using the photo as a guide. Again cut the lace motifs into four and place one across each corner and iron over the scalloped lace.

11 Use the silk ribbon and the tapestry needle to embroider clusters of French knots in the gray/mauve ribbon. Use a lazy daisy stitch for the leaves referring to the photo as guide to positions around the print and in the scalloped lace. See page 92 for stitches.

12 Use the beading needle and thread to sew three seed pearls in the center of each pansy.

13 Use the beading needle, thread and antique glass seed beads to bead the lattice, the butterfly and the lace using the photo as guide to position and colors. Now frame your picture.

Pansy Print Framed in Lace

❧⋅❧

This project uses basic sewing by hand and machine to achieve maximum effect proving that something doesn't have to be difficult to look amazing. Take pansy design No 1003 printed on moiré taffeta, back it with batting, embroider the print design, then outline and stipple quilt the fabric print. Add more fabric, lace and beading and the results are simply stunning.

MATERIALS

- Victorian print No 1003 on antique colored moiré taffeta
- 25.5cm (10in) square of Pellon H640/fusible batting
- 48cm (19in) square of plain fabric to match or contrast the print fabric
- 4 narrow lace corner pieces to be antique dyed (page 82)
- 4 wide lace corner pieces to be dyed (page 82)
- 2 lace motifs to be antique dyed (page 82), cut into four pieces to complete the lace surround
- 3 packets of antique seed beads in green luster, purple luster and pink glass
- 9 seed pearls
- 1 beading needle and thread
- Rayon 40 embroidery thread 1 reel each of: black/purple, gray/mauve, golden yellow, orange rust, warm brown/green , black/green, olive green, light beige, white and gold metallic
- Pre-wound bobbins
- Silk embroidery ribbon in green and mauve
- Tapestry needle to suit the above
- 50cm (20in) Vliesofix/Wonderunder
- 50cm (20in) self-adhesive tear-away stabilizer
- Machine feet: open-toe embroidery foot and clear-view freehand embroidery foot
- Size 80/90 large-eyed needle
- Jenny Haskins Pfaff Choice card or three lace butterflies
- 450 craft glue or similar clear flexible craft glue
- General sewing requirements

PREPARATION

1 Iron the Pellon/fusible batting to the back of the pansy print.

2 Dye all lace pieces using the potassium permanganate dyeing technique on page 82 then iron Vliesofix/Wonderunder to the back of the pieces using the technique on page 84 and put to one side.

3 Use the gold metallic thread, a pre-wound bobbin and the open-toe foot to:

—quilt the lattice in the center of the heart, using stitch No 01 length 1.5

—outline the heart with a narrow satin stitch, width 1.5

—stitch No 50 narrow width and length on the outside of the satin stitch.

4 Use the gray/mauve thread to embroider six scattered, small flowers from your built-in stitches, using the single pattern button to sew one flower at a time then move the fabric to a new position. Use the open-toe embroidery foot, pre-wound bobbin and size 80/90 large-eyed needle.

QUILTING

5 Lower the feed dogs, use the clear-view freehand embroidery foot, straight stitch and threads from the materials list that best match those used, to outline quilt the pansies and leaves. Accent the 'cheeks' and 'beard' and some shading on the pansies with freehand embroidery, matching threads to the colors on the pansies and leaves. (Use the close-up photo as a guide.)

6 Use the light beige thread to stipple-quilt the area surrounding the print.

7 Trim the fabric edges of the print to measure 25.5cm (10in) square, then pin it to the center of the backing fabric and straight stitch around all sides, close to the fabric edges.

8 Position the four large lace corner pieces so they cover the corners of the print then cut the lace motif into four suitable sections to fill in the gap between the corner pieces. Place the raw ends of these lace pieces under one corner piece and over the other to give a creeper effect. When happy with the design, iron in place.

✂ TIP ✂ You may choose to freehand straight stitch around the outside edge of the lace pieces, but as the piece is being framed it is not necessary.

EMBROIDERY

8 Use the self-adhesive tear-away technique on page 86 to embroider three small butterflies from the Pfaff Jenny Haskins Choice card in warm brown/green thread (refer to the photo for positions).

✂ TIP ✂ Beading and hand embroidery are relaxing and can be done anywhere, so hand bead and embroider at your leisure.

9 Use the photo as guide, silk ribbon and a tapestry needle to hand embroider the following:

—clusters of French knots using the gray mauve ribbon

—scattered leaves using the lazy daisy stitch and green ribbon, around the French knots and as accents in the lace (see page 92).

10 Use the photo as a guide, the beading needle and thread, to bead the center print and add accents to the lace. Follow the colors used or make up your own designs and color schemes.

The embellished print is now ready to be framed. You may choose a wonderful fabric to cover the board that surrounds the print or just plain board; it is up to you. The four small lace corner pieces and the ribbon and bead cluster pin were attached after the print was framed using 450 craft glue.

Framed Pansy Basket

Machine embroidery can be integrated into any technique, adding to the artist's work. Such is the case with this project. A machine-embroidered basket with a bow on the handle and butterfly form the foundation of this Victorian picture. Against a background of amethyst silk, the basket, trimmed with hand painted lace, holds a typical Victorian posy of ribbon pansies and roses and enamel pansy buttons. The larger pansies are made with shaded wired ribbon that is flipped when making the second set of petals, the 'cheeks' and 'beard' trio, for an intriguing color variation. Beading the butterfly and adding a circular lace edged mount complete the picture.

MATERIALS

- 40cm (1/2yd) of amethyst satin background fabric
- 40cm (1/2yd) Pellon H640/fusible batting
- 1.2m x 19mm (1 1/3yd x 3/4in) shaded purple wired ribbon for larger pansies
- 1.2m x 19mm (1 1/3yd x 3/4in) shaded plum wired ribbon for larger pansies
- 80cm x 13mm (7/8yd x 1/2in) light blue grosgrain ribbon for smaller pansies
- 1m x 7mm (1 1/8yd x 1/4in) yellow silk ribbon for pansy centers
- 60cm x 25mm (2/3yd x 1in) green wired ribbon for pansy leaves
- 20cm (8in) buckram for backing pansies
- 20cm x 13mm (12in x 1/2in) each of purple, blue/purple and slate green satin ribbon for roses
- 3 enamel pansy buttons
- Seed beads in cream and amethyst
- Beading needle and thread
- 70 cm (3/4yd) old dark cream deep scalloped edging lace to edge the mount

- Rayon lace motif, hand painted (see page 83)
- Rayon 40 embroidery threads, one reel each of: black/purple, dusky purple, golden green, warm brown/green
- Size 80/90 machine embroidery needle
- 1 pre-wound bobbin or Bobbinfil
- PC-design software
- Blank memory card
- Victorian Bows and Baskets embroidery disk formatted for all brands of machine for bow
- Baskets embroidery disk by Cactus Punch formatted for all brands of sewing machine for basket
- Jenny Haskins Pfaff Choice card for butterfly
- Self-adhesive tear-away
- Spray adhesive
- 450 craft glue or similar clear flexible craft glue
- 40cm square of mat board
- HB pencil
- Craft knife or scalpel
- Compass
- General sewing requirements

PREPARATION

1 From the amethyst satin, cut:
— two, 40cm (16in) squares.
From the Pellon/fusible batting, cut:
—one 40cm (16in) square, then fuse this
to the wrong side of one amethyst satin
square.

2 Fold the batting-backed square
vertically then horizontally
through the middle; meeting
point of folds is the center. At this
point scribe a circle with 10cm (4in)
radius (20cm [8in] diameter) using
pencil and compass.

3 Scribe a circle the same size in the center of the
mat board. Cut out circle carefully with a craft knife
or scalpel. Lightly spray one side of the board and
the wrong side of the unbacked piece of satin with
adhesive and press them together. Cut away most of
the fabric within the circle, leaving 2.5cm (1in) for
turning. Clip the turning allowance at 1cm (^{3}/8in)
intervals, and press through to the other side of the
mat board with fingers. Set aside.

4 Refer to page 83 to hand paint the lace motif in
colors to match the thread colors.

MACHINE EMBROIDERY

✄ NOTE ✄ Use the self-adhesive tear-away
technique on page 86, pre-wound bobbin, rayon 40
embroidery thread and a size 80/90 embroidery
needle for all machine embroidery.

5 Using the PC-design software download
the basket and bow from their respective
disks onto the blank memory card. The
butterfly is from the Jenny Haskins
Choice Card.

6 Refer to photo for
placement of machine
embroidery within the
pencil-marked circle. Basket
is slightly off center and to the
left. Butterfly is at two o'clock.
Embroider the basket in warm
brown/green and golden green
threads then position an angled bow
off center on the basket handle and
embroider with the purple shades
of thread. Butterfly is embroidered
in warm brown/green thread.

RIBBON FLOWERS AND LEAVES

✄ TIP ✄ To achieve a more
realistic effect with variation between the two sets
of petals in each pansy, flip the shaded wired ribbon
after making the first 'ear' set. You could have bi-
color pansies with different back and front petals .

7 Make three purple, three plum and three blue
pansies using the corresponding ribbons and
buckram from the materials list and following the
technique on page 92.

8 Make folded ribbon roses from the three pieces
of satin ribbon following technique on page 92.

9 Cut green wired ribbon into three 20cm (8in)
lengths. Make pleated, scrunched leaves (see page
93 for the technique).

10 You may choose to either stitch or glue the
pansies, roses, leaves, and buttons to form a spray in
the embroidered basket. Use the photo as guide to
positioning.

11 Use the beading needle and thread to bead the
butterfly with cream and amethyst seed beads.

FINISHING

12 Glue the lace motif over basket base.

13 To elevate the mount from the pansy picture
prior to framing, glue a small folded piece of paper
to each underside corner of the covered mat board.

14 Glue the edging lace around the circle of the mat
board, positioning lace to match the pattern at the
join. You may need to clip between the scallops to
ensure the lace sits flat. Your picture is now ready to
be framed.

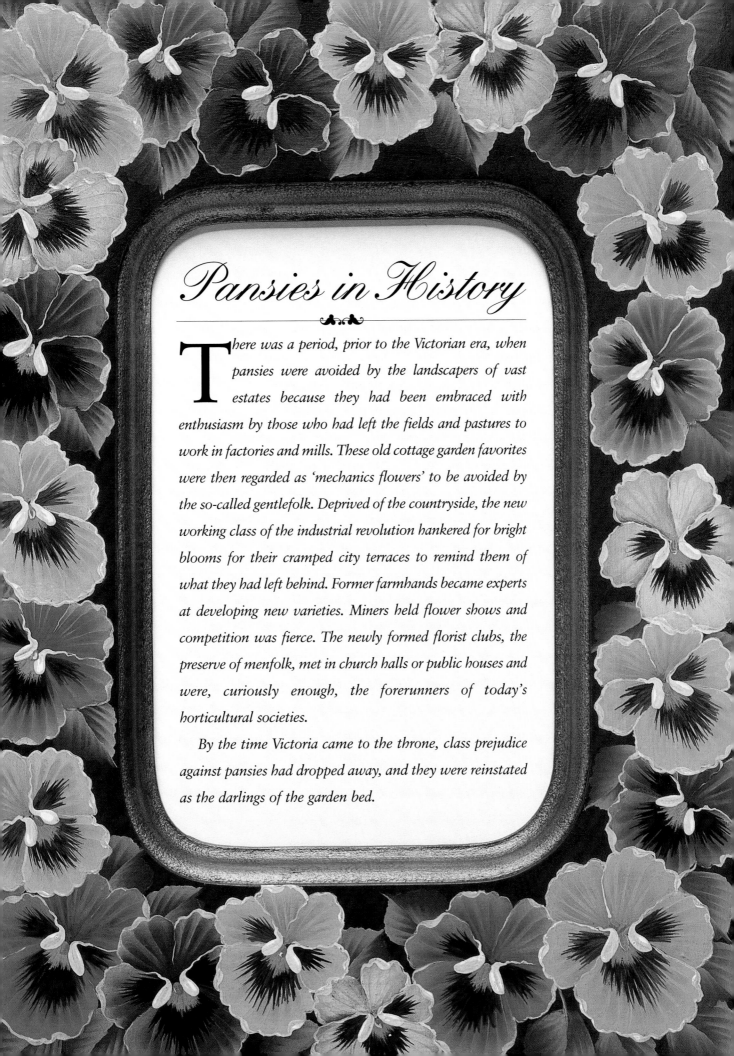

Pansies in History

There was a period, prior to the Victorian era, when pansies were avoided by the landscapers of vast estates because they had been embraced with enthusiasm by those who had left the fields and pastures to work in factories and mills. These old cottage garden favorites were then regarded as 'mechanics flowers' to be avoided by the so-called gentlefolk. Deprived of the countryside, the new working class of the industrial revolution hankered for bright blooms for their cramped city terraces to remind them of what they had left behind. Former farmhands became experts at developing new varieties. Miners held flower shows and competition was fierce. The newly formed florist clubs, the preserve of menfolk, met in church halls or public houses and were, curiously enough, the forerunners of today's horticultural societies.

By the time Victoria came to the throne, class prejudice against pansies had dropped away, and they were reinstated as the darlings of the garden bed.

Pins & Purses Evening Bag

Construct a unique evening bag, a stunning replica of a Victorian purse, following the simple step-by-step instructions. Using cardboard, glue and a little ingenuity this purse is easily achieved in a matter of hours. The Victorian pin adds the finishing touch, reminiscent of a time when dressing was an art form and the process of matching shoes, bag and gloves for every outfit was essential for a lady of impeccable taste and character.

Purse

MATERIALS

- 30cm x 115cm (12in x 45in) black fabric such as silk dupion or satin
- 30cm x 115 cm (12in x 45in) black lining fabric
- 30cm x 94cm (12in x 34in) Pellon H640/fusible batting
- 1.4 m (1¹/2yd) black cord for shoulder strap
- 10cm (4in) heavy interfacing
- 1 reel black construction thread
- Machine needles: size 75 universal needle, size 80 and 100 jeans needle
- Machine feet: normal sewing foot and zipper foot
- Sheet of light weight cardboard
- Tracing paper
- 450 craft glue or similar clear flexible craft glue
- Craft spray glue
- 1 set black Velcro® dots or suitable fastener
- 1 black tassel either purchased or make your own
- Hand sewing needle
- Long strong pins
- Pegs/clothes pins
- HB pencil
- Chalk pencil
- General sewing requirements

PREPARATION

✄ TIP ✄ Label all pattern, cardboard and fabric pieces to clearly identify them when putting the purse together.

Use tracing paper and HB pencil to trace the purse pattern pieces from the pattern sheet, marking all lines, then cut them out. These are used to cut the cardboard, the purse fabric and lining, Pellon/fusible batting and heavy weight interfacing.

1 From the light weight cardboard cut:
—one purse front and back, cutting on the seamline except the lower edge
—two flaps, cutting on the seamline
—two bases, cutting on the seamline
—one lining, cutting on the seamline except the lower edge.

2 From the black purse fabric cut:
—one purse front, back, base and flap, two gussets.

3 From the black lining fabric cut:
—one wrap-around front/back, flap, base, two gussets and one strip for attaching the strap.

4 From the heavy interfacing cut:
—two gussets
—one strip for attaching the strap
—one flap with seam allowances trimmed away.

5 From the Pellon/fusible batting cut:
—one purse flap, front, back and one base cutting along the seamline.

✄ TIP ✄ Fit all pieces before gluing to ensure an accurate fit. Make any adjustments to the fabric pattern pieces before applying them to the cardboard shapes and gluing in place.

6 Iron the Pellon/fusible batting to the wrong side of fabric front, back, base and flap.

7 Fuse or tack the heavy interfacing to the strip, gussets and bag flap.

8 Snip lower seam allowance of back, front and lining card at 1cm (¹/2in) intervals. Score lower seam lines to make folding of seam allowance easier.

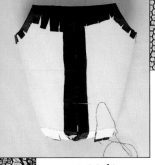

*1. Making
the lining.*

*2. Making
the gussets.*

*3. Gussets glued
to lining.*

*4. Positioning cord
on flap lining.*

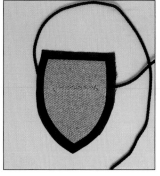

*5. Strip is stitched
to flap lining.*

*6. Underside of
flap lining.*

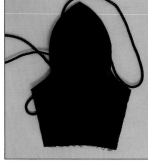

*7. Covering the front
and back.*

*8. Topstitching
flap to back.*

*9. Front and back
pinned together.*

*10. Preparing purse and
lining bases.*

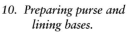

PUTTING IT TOGETHER
Inner Bag

✂ T I P ✂ When using spray glue, do it in a well-ventilated space where the spray and fumes can be contained. Do it inside a large box but take the box out of doors.

9 Lightly spray the back of the lining fabric for the inside of the purse then center the cardboard pattern piece over the fabric and hand press removing any creases or bubbles. Clip the fabric edges on all sides except the center back seam, then turn the fabric to the back and hold in place with the craft glue. Secure the center back seam (cardboard outside, lining fabric inside) with a hand sewing needle and a slipstitch. Repeat for the base turning under and gluing all fabric edges. See photograph 1.

10 Use the construction thread, normal sewing foot and size 75 universal needle to sew the darts in the gusset pieces. Then sew the purse and lining gusset pieces together around the top curved edge. Clip the seam, turn to the right side, press and top stitch this seam. Clip the lower edge of the gusset (with dart). Repeat for second gusset. See photograph 2.

11 Glue the gussets to each side of the cardboard lining piece matching the curves on the side of the purse lining to the bottom curve of the gussets. See photograph 3.

Purse flaps and handle

12 Spray-glue the Pellon/fusible batting side of the purse flap then center the cardboard pattern piece over the Pellon/fusible batting, clip the edges and turn to the wrong side to glue.

13 Iron the edges to the wrong side around the strip for attaching the purse cord, then use the chalk pencil to mark the strip position on the flap lining and pin, encasing the raw ends of the cord handle. See photograph 4.

14 Use the construction thread and a size 80 jeans needle to stitch around all sides of the fabric strip; this will secure the cord handle. See photographs 5 and 6.

15 Spray glue the heavy interfacing on the back of the lining flap, center the cardboard pattern piece over the interfacing, clip the edges then turn to the wrong side and glue. Center the front flap over the lining flap, making sure all sides match and are even, then glue together. (If you choose to have a black tassel on the point of the flap then insert it between the two flaps at this point of constructing the purse.)

Purse front and back

16 Lightly spray glue the Pellon/fusible batting side of the front and back purse fabric pieces then center the cardboard pattern pieces over the batting. Clip all sides of the fabric except the straight side seams. Turn the top clipped edges to the back and glue. See photograph 7.

17 Pin the flap, where marked on the purse, to the back then use construction thread and a size 100 jeans needle to top stitch the flap to the purse back with a double row of stitching. See photograph 8.

18 Apply glue to the front lining piece of the purse around the edges and in the center. Overlay the purse front on the purse lining, matching the top of the pieces then use pegs/clothes pins to hold it all in place. Overlap the side seams with the seam allowance fabric on either side of the purse front, pulling the fabric and pinning securely so the front is firm and flat. Allow the glue to set for about 15 minutes before removing pins. Fold under the side seams of the purse back and glue, then repeat the above for the back of the purse with the flap attached. Make sure there is no cardboard showing on the side seams. Should the side seams not meet exactly, cover any discrepancy with a flat black braid before finishing the purse. See photograph 9.

19 Spray glue the bases cut from purse and lining fabric. Center the cardboard pattern pieces over the fabric, press together by hand, clip the edges then turn seam allowances of fabrics to the wrong side and glue in place. See photograph 10.

20 Apply glue to the complete under surface of the base and lining. Squeeze the purse into the shape that exactly fits the base shape then press the base to the bottom of the purse, pinning around all the edges to hold in place and shape until the glue dries. Press the lining base to the bottom of the inside of the purse making sure it is flat and smooth.

21 Glue a Velcro® dot on the underside of the flap and a corresponding position on the front of the purse as a closure.

Remove all pins and pegs (clothes pins) before the glue completely dries. Allow glue to set for 24 hours before using the purse.

Victorian Pin

There are many ways to make a Victorian pin, but basically the print is backed with batting and covers a cardboard heart shape which is edged with trimmings. Ribbon leaves, fabric leaves, pleated ribbon and threaded drop beads are glued to the back of the print then a felt heart shape covers the raw fabric edges and is where the clip is positioned. This is a great project to use up those little scrap pieces of fabric, ribbon and trims that are too good to throw away. Other alternatives are machine embroidery motifs, ribbon pansies or an antique clip as the center of your Victorian pin.

MATERIALS

- Victorian heart print No 1008 petite
- 35cm x 45mm (14in x 1³/4in) each of variegated green and pink-green wire-edged ribbon (ribbon leaves and pleated ribbon)
- 75cm x 6mm (30in x ¹/4in) antique grosgrain ribbon (small pansies)
- 20cm x 25mm (8in x 1in) gold edging braid
- 30cm (12in) narrow gold metallic cord
- 30cm x 20mm (12in x ³/4in) olive green edging braid
- 3 small hand painted lace flowers
- Small antique button and butterfly
- 2 variegated velvet leaves
- Beading needle and thread
- Seed beads
- 10cm (4in) square of light weight batting
- 10cm (4in) square of felt
- 10cm (4in) square of medium weight cardboard
- 7.5cm x 90mm (3in x 3¹/2in) antique drop bead ribbon (beaded ribbon that can be bought by the metre/yard or you can make your own using glass seed and bugle beads).
- 450 craft glue or similar clear flexible craft glue
- Craft spray glue
- Hand sewing needle and thread
- Brooch clip
- General sewing requirements

PREPARATION

1 Refer to page 94 in the techniques section to make three leaves using the 35cm (14in) green variegated wire edged ribbon.

2 Refer to page 92 in the techniques section to make two small pansies using the narrow grosgrain ribbon. As a center detail, sew three small glass seed beads using beading needle and thread to the center of each pansy.

3 Trace the heart shape from the print to the cardboard, then cut out the heart shape along the seam line. Trace this heart on the batting and felt then cut out the two heart shapes.

4 Lightly spray-glue the back of the silk print and center the batting heart over the silk heart then cut out the silk heart 1cm (5/8in) from the seamline and clip all sides back to within 1mm (1/16in) of the seamline.

5 Lightly spray-glue the cardboard heart shape, center it over the back of the batting then turn the raw edges of the silk heart to the back and glue in place using craft glue.

6 Glue the olive green edging braid to the back of the heart then glue the narrow-gold cord around the edge of the heart from the front, so the gold cord sits over the olive-green edging braid.

7 Pleat up the pink/green wired ribbon to measure 12.5cm (5 1/2in) then glue from the back around the top of the heart. Make the pleats tighter at the bottom near the heart so the ribbon slightly fans out at the top. Glue the gold edging braid to the back at the top of the fanned out ribbon, to hold the pleats in place.

8 From the back, glue the three previously made wire edged ribbon leaves to the left of the heart and the two velvet leaves to the right of the heart, making sure they face in different directions. Glue the drop beads to the bottom point at the back of the heart

9 Glue the two small pansies, the butterfly, lace flowers and antique button to the front of the pin, using the photo as a guide.

10 Glue the felt heart to the back of the pin covering the raw fabric edges. Hand sew then glue the brooch clip to the center back of the pin. Allow to dry for 24 hours before using the clip.

Clip the pin to the center front of the purse flap to complete this romantic purse.

Lady-in-Waiting Quilt

Framing shapes including ovals, a diamond and a rounded square surrounding the print of a gracious Victorian lady give a stately presence to this quilted wall hanging. Embellished with machine embroidered bows, butterflies and pansies as well as lace segments, quilting and decorative machine stitching, all these techniques and devices work their special kind of magic here. Instructions are for a wall hanging, but add a series of blocks on all sides, selecting motifs and methods befitting the main subject, and this project could easily convert to a quilt possessing heirloom status.

MATERIALS

- 1m (1¹/8yd) antique white quilters muslin
- 1m (1¹/8yd) backing fabric
- 1.3m (1¹/2yd) printed fabric for straight border
- 1.3m (1¹/2yd) contrast fabric for scalloped border overlay
- 1.3m (1¹/2yd) batting
- 25cm (10in) white organza for free-standing embroidered butterflies
- Victorian quilt prints, one of each in medium 1014, 1003 and 1004
- 1.3m (1¹/2yd) Vliesofix/Wonderunder
- Appliqué mat
- 1.5m (1²/3yd) non-adhesive tear-away fabric stabilizer
- 50cm (¹/2yd) self-adhesive tear-away
- 25cm (10in) melt-away plastic stabilizer
- PC-design software
- Blank memory card
- Victorian Scrolls and Curlicues and Victorian Pansies embroidery disks formatted for all brands of sewing machines
- Jenny Haskins Pfaff Choice card for organza butterflies
- Rayon 40 embroidery threads in 8 colors of your choice which match the quilt prints and border fabrics
- Bobbinfil or two pre-wound bobbins
- 1 reel of construction thread
- 2 reels 60 denier heirloom thread to match the main quilt fabric – cream
- 1 reel of monofilament thread
- Machine feet: open-toe foot, quarter-inch quilting foot and clear-view freehand embroidery foot
- Machine needles: size 80 embroidery needle, size 75 universal needle ditch quilting and construction and size 60/80 needle for quilting
- Quilters ruler, rotary cutter and board
- 2H pencil
- Large piece of brown paper for making the oval template
- 4 cream corner rayon lace motifs for lace motifs for the center of the quilt
- 3 lace butterflies
- General sewing requirements

FINISHED SIZE OF QUILT
34in x 44in.

PREPARATION

In keeping with the traditions of quilting, all measurements in the method are Imperial.

1 From the background fabric cut:
—one, 25in x 34in rectangle.

2 From the border fabric cut:
—four, 6in wide strips across the width of the fabric.
Cut the above into:
—two, 34¹/2in lengths top and bottom border
—two, 32¹/2in lengths side borders.
—five, 2¹/2in strips the width of fabric for binding.

3 Iron Vliesofix/Wonderunder to the back of the border overlay fabric before cutting.
From the border overlay fabric cut:
—four, 3in strips the length of the fabric.
Cut the above into:
—two, strips 45in long
—two, strips 35in long.

4 Iron Vliesofix/Wonderunder to the back of the three quilt prints. Cut around the lady oval and the pansy leaves at the bottom of the oval. Cut around the outside edge of the heart and pansy shapes as you would for appliqué.

5 Use the quarter oval from the pattern sheet as a template to make an oval from the brown paper. Cut a piece of brown paper a little larger than the backing fabric dimensions. Fold the paper into quarters. Place the quarter oval template over the folded paper, matching the folded edges to the straight edges of the template and trace around the curved line. Cut along this line with the paper still folded.

6 Fold the backing fabric in the same way to find the center of the rectangle, and finger press the folds. Unfold the brown paper and lay it over the backing fabric matching the centers and all fold lines. Draw around the edge of the oval with the 2H pencil. This oval will act as a guide to placement of embroidery and quilt prints. Refer to diagram No 1 on the pattern sheet.

7 Remove the paper from the back of the quilt prints then use an appliqué mat to iron the prints in place using diagram No 1 as a guide.

EMBROIDERY
Built-in Guided Stitches
✂ TIP ✂ Use tear-away stabilizer at the back of all guided machine embroidery.

8 Use the open-toe embroidery foot, size 80 embroidery needle, pre-wound bobbin, rayon 40 embroidery thread and stitch No 60 width and length 6.0 and density 0.25 to appliqué around the edges of the three quilt prints. The embroidery thread should match the straight border fabric in color.

9 Use a small circular plate to draw curves around each quarter of the oval lady. See diagram No 2 on pattern sheet.

10 Use cream thread, the size 75 Universal needle, and a triple stitch to sew a half-inch diagonal grid within each of these areas. Repeat step No 8 with dark cream thread to stitch around the four inner curved lines. See diagram No 2.

11 Position corner lace motifs at the top, bottom and sides of the center oval lady and stitch in place with matching thread and a freehand stitch using the clear-view embroidery foot.

12 Use a contrasting thread and an open scallop to stitch around the outside edge of stitch No 60 on the inner curves, stopping and starting at the lace motifs at the top and bottom.

13 Join the inside edge of the lace motifs by sewing stitch No 60, width and length 6.0 and density 0.25 with dark cream thread, stopping and starting at the edge of the lace motifs. Refer to diagram No 2.
Embroidery Motifs
Note: For easy accurate placement, refer to page 86 for the self-adhesive tear-away embroidery technique used for all motif embroidery.

14 Use the PC-design software to down load the pansy spray from Victorian Pansies design disk, and the large bow from Victorian Scrolls and Curlicues to a blank memory card.

15 Use the photo and diagram No 1 as a guide to embroidery placement and embroider three pansy sprays (minus the buds and fronds) at the top and both sides of the large oval, in colors that best match the prints and fabric. Embroider the large bow at the bottom of the large oval.

16 Use the same equipment as in step 8 matching rayon 40 embroidery thread to the outer border fabric and an embroidered leaf stitch to connect the large oval and the embroidery designs.

17 Refer to page 86 of the techniques section to embroider two butterflies from Jenny Haskins Choice card on the organza over the melt-away, then cut them out.

BORDERS

18 Remove all excess stabilizer from the back of the embroidery, press the center rectangle flat then trim to a 23 1/2in x 32 1/2in rectangle.

19 Attach the 6in x 32 1/2in border strips to the sides of the center rectangle and then the 6in x 34 1/2in border strips to the top and bottom using construction thread in the needle and bobbin, size 75 universal needle and the quarter-inch foot.

20 Using the overlay border fabric and referring to the mitered corner technique on page 89 make a frame of fabric with outside dimensions matching those of the constructed wall hanging.

21 To plot the scallops on the fabric frame, use each corner as a starting and finishing point. Divide the inside long side of the rectangle into six equal sections and the inside short side into four equal sections. Use a small saucer to mark even scallops that exactly fit the marked sections.

22 Mark 1 1/2in from the outside edge on each corner along the miter line. Extend a scallop on either side of the inside mitered corners, then connect these with a curved shape with its mid point on the marked line. Refer to the photo and diagram No 3 on the pattern sheet as a guide, then cut along the scalloped lines.

23 Remove the paper from the back of the scalloped fabric frame then position it over the border fabric, matching sides and corners accurately, then iron in place.

24 Using the techniques, same stitch and thread as in step No 8, embroider around the scallops to appliqué the overlay frame fabric in place.

QUILTING

25 Cut out the backing fabric and batting 3in larger on all sides than the finished wall hanging. Sandwich the batting between the quilt top and bottom, and starting at the center, secure at 4in intervals with small safety pins,.

26 Anchor your quilt by ditch-quilting in the long straight seam lines, using monofilament thread and the size 75 universal needle and matching bobbin thread to the quilt backing.

27 With the 60 denier thread to match the quilt top, thread in the bobbin to match the quilt backing and the clear-view freehand foot, stipple-quilt inside the large oval and in the small space around the oval quilt print between the lace and the print.

28 Use the open-toe embroidery foot with the above threads and needle to quilt the area outside the large oval with a double diagonal cross hatch straight stitch. Use the width of the foot for distance and accuracy of the double row of quilting. Refer to the photo as a guide.

BINDING

29 Join the 2 1/2in strips for the binding into one long strip then fold in half lengthways, wrong sides together, and press. Position the quilt binding on the quilt top with right sides together and aligning the raw edges of the binding and quilt top. Use the quarter-inch foot and construction thread and needle to sew the binding to the quilt through all layers, mitering the corners as you sew and joining the binding with a turned-under overlap. Turn binding to the wrong side of the quilt, press and pin, then hand sew to the back of the quilt.

30 Use the photo as guide for placement of the three lace butterflies and the embroidered organza butterflies and stitch in place with monofilament thread leaving the organza butterflies free-standing. Sign and date your quilt/wall hanging.

Pansy Boudoir
Hanger

A silk coat hanger, embellished with printed and ribbon pansies then further enhanced with ribbon embroidery and dripping with old gold lace, is a small but lavishly ornate indulgence in today's busy, streamlined world. It is also a fine example of the Victorian art of turning something mundane into a thing of beauty. Reserve this coat hanger for a special ensemble in your wardrobe, make one for a bride for her wedding dress or scale the pattern down and create a smaller version for a christening gown.

MATERIALS

- 30cm (1/3yd) cream silk taffeta
- 30cm (1/3yd) Pellon H640/fusible batting
- Victorian pansy print No 1003 large
- 5m x 100mm (5¹/₂yd x 4in) antique dyed edging lace (see page 82) to drop from the bottom of the coat hanger
- 50cm x 25mm (²/₃yd x 1in) green shaded organza ribbon for leaves
- 50cm x 25mm (²/₃yd x 1in) gold organza ribbon for bow
- 1.5m x 25mm (2²/₃yd x 1in) purple wired ribbon for pansies
- 30cm x 7mm (12in x ¹/₄in) yellow silk ribbon for center of pansies
- 1 hank of 4mm (1/8in) Thread Gatherer silk ribbon, color Egyptian Nights or 4-5m x 4mm (4-5yd x 1/8in) variegated silk ribbon in shades of pink-purple for hand embroidered silk ribbon flowers
- 2m x 4mm (1¹/4yd x ¹/8in) yellow silk ribbon for the center of the embroidered flowers
- 1 tapestry needle for silk ribbon embroidery
- 1.2m (1¹/3yd) gold insertion cord with flange to edge the coat hanger
- 25cm (10in) Vliesofix/Wonderunder
- Construction thread
- Size 75 universal machine needle
- Zipper foot
- Hand sewing needle
- Wooden coat hanger
- Small amount of Toyfill
- General sewing requirements

PREPARATION

1 Allowing sufficient silk taffeta fabric for the front and back of the hanger, cut a bias piece measuring 20cm x 2.5cm (8in x 1in) for covering the hook.

2 Iron Pellon/fusible batting to the back of the remaining silk taffeta fabric, fold in two and using the pattern from the pattern sheet, cut two cover pieces using a fabric marking pen to mark the openings.

3 Iron Vliesofix (Wonderunder) to the back of the pansy print, cut out pansies then peel away backing paper and iron the pansies into position on the coat hanger front.

METHOD

4 Make two pansies and five leaves with the purple wired and green shaded organza ribbon (see pages 92 and 94 respectively for the techniques).

5 Following the placement pattern on the pattern sheet, refer to page 92 to ribbon stitch small flowers around the printed pansies using the tapestry needle and the 'Egyptian Nights' silk ribbon. Use the yellow silk ribbon to embroider French knots in the center of each flower.

6 Use the photo as a guide to placement of the silk pansies and leaves, stitching the leaves in place, then the pansies.

7 Pin the insertion cord (starting and finishing at one lower corner) to the right side of the coat hanger front, aligning the straight edge of the flange with the raw edges of the fabric, and pin. Unravel cord ends and re-weave both strand ends together to disguise the join. With construction thread in the size 75 universal needle and using the zipper foot and needle positions, stitch close to the cord as with piping.

8 Join the wide dyed edging lace into a circle then gather it to fit the bottom edge of the front of coat hanger cover, as marked on the pattern sheet. Align the straight edges of the gathered lace to the raw fabric edge/cord flange of the lower edge of the

coat hanger front, and pin. Stitch into place using the zipper foot and needle positions to ensure the lace is stitched close to the edge of the cord.

9 Pin up the gathered lace so it lies flat against the coat hanger front, making sure it is away from all seams. Lay the coat hanger back over the front, right sides together (as with making a cushion) and pin, then use the zipper foot and needle positions to sew the two pieces together leaving the openings as marked on the pattern sheet.

10 Clip the curved edges and turn to the right side, unpinning the lace so it falls free. Remove the hook from the coat hanger and insert wooden part in the cover, aligning the hole in the coat hanger for the hook with the matching opening in the cover. Screw the hook into the coat hanger.

11 Fill the coat hanger with Toyfill – do not over stuff.

✂ TIP ✂ You may choose to place some lavender in with the stuffing to add a soft perfume to keep clothes sweet smelling.

12 Use the hand-sewing needle to sew the turning opening closed with a small slipstitch.

13 Fold the bias silk strip in half lengthwise, right sides together, press and sew a 7mm (1/4in) seam down the length and across one short end. Clip the corner, trim seam and turn through to right side. Measure this tube on the coat hanger hook and cut to fit. Slip over hook and hand stitch to the cover.

14 Use the gold organza ribbon to tie a bow around the base of the hook to complete this extravagant boudoir coat hanger.

Pansy Bell Pull

A cord was used to summon servants from their quarters at the bidding of the master or mistress. Cords connected to bells in the servants quarters, were strategically placed throughout the house. When the cord was pulled, the bell that rang indicated the room in which the servant was required. Elaborate tapestries and needlework were used to cover these cords, hence the name 'bell pull'. Today, bell pulls are used as charming wall hangings; a constant reminder of gracious past times.

MATERIALS

- *30cm (12in) floral pansy fabric*
- *25cm (10in) Pellon H640/fusible batting*
- *3 small quilt prints No 1008a*
- *1 small quilt print No 1003*
- *1.5m (1⁵⁄₈ yd) olive green satin piping*
- *1.5m x 50mm (1⁵⁄₈yd x 2in) deep scalloped edging lace dyed purple*
- *1.5m x 20mm (1⁵⁄₈yd x ³⁄₄in) antique edging lace*
- *Rayon 40 embroidery thread, one reel each of: light mauve, dusky purple and dark olive green*
- *1 reel metallic gold thread*
- *1 reel of construction thread*
- *1 reel of monofilament thread*
- *Pre-wound bobbins or Bobbinfil*
- *Jenny Haskins Pfaff Choice card*
- *Size 80/90 machine embroidery needle*
- *Machine feet: clear-view freehand embroidery foot, quarter-inch foot, zipper foot and open-toe embroidery foot*
- *25cm (10in) tear-away fabric stabilizer*
- *50cm (20in) self-adhesive tear-away stabilizer*
- *General sewing requirements*

PREPARATION

1 From the floral pansy fabric cut:
—one, 61cm x 19cm (24in x 7¹⁄₂in) rectangle for the backing
—two, 5cm (2in) strips across the width of the fabric for sashing and border strips.
From the above cut:
—two, 56cm (22in) border strips
—four, 13cm (5in) sashing strips

2 Cut the four quilt prints to measure 13.5cm x 12cm (5¹⁄₄in x 4³⁄₄in) making sure the prints are centered in each rectangle.

3 Cut a 61cm x 19cm (24in x 7¹⁄₂in) rectangle from the Pellon/fusible batting.

JOINING THE SASHING AND BORDERS

4 Use construction thread and the quarter-inch foot to joint the four quilt prints with the floral sashing into one strip, starting with a sashing strip and finishing with a print.

5 Join the border strips to either side of the sashed print strip. Press all seams to the center.

6 Use tear-away stabilizer, the size 80/90 embroidery needle, pre-wound bobbin, open-toe embroidery foot and olive green rayon 40 embroidery thread to sew a border around each quilt print using stitch No 60, width and length 6.0 and density 0.25. Face the scallop to the center of the print and align the straight edge with the edge of the print.

7 Use the self-adhesive tear-away technique on page 86 to embroidery small butterflies from Jenny Haskins Choice card, in the top left corner of each print. Referring to the photo as a guide for position and color use the metallic gold thread for two butterflies and shades of purple rayon 40 embroidery thread for the other two.

CONSTRUCTION

8 Iron the Pellon/fusible batting to the back of the embroidered bell pull. Cut the print end of the bell pull into a rounded 'V' shape using the photo as a guide to size and shape. Cut the backing fabric to the same shape.

9 Use the zipper foot, construction thread and needle positions to sew the olive green satin piping to the edge of the bell pull. Then sew the narrow edging lace over the top of the piping. A third layer, the purple deep scalloped edging lace, is sewn over the narrow edging lace.

10 Place the backing fabric over the front of the bell pull with right sides together (as for a cushion), pin then sew starting and finishing on either side of the top sashing strip using the zipper foot and appropriate needle positions to sew close to the piping.

11 Turn to the right side then turn the seam allowances of the top opening in, pin, then press all seams flat.

12 Use stitch No 01, the zipper foot and gold metallic thread to top stitch around all sides of the bell pull, close to the piping and closing the top turning opening at the same time.

QUILTING

13 Use the open-toe foot and monofilament thread to ditch-stitch in all straight seam lines.

14 Lower the feed dogs, use the clear-view freehand foot, monofilament thread in the needle and bobbin thread to match the backing fabric to outline quilt the pansy designs on the quilt prints.

15 Gold metallic thread is used to stipple-quilt the unembellished background fabric of the prints with small continuous meandering figure eights which never overlap.

You may choose to purchase a metal bell pull attachment to complete your bell pull, or make up your own with a bar at the top and a tassel at the bottom.

Techniques

Apply the three 'Ps' practice, patience and perseverance to the mastering of the techniques listed and explained on these pages. For the machine and hand sewer, techniques are like the brush strokes of an artist – the better you are at the basics, the easier the art form becomes, but it doesn't just happen. Here you will find some tips, tricks, techniques and ideas that will enhance both hand and machine embroidery along with easy ways to miter corners and bind quilts as well as some fabric painting advice and several explanations of ribbon work.

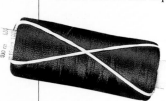

Reels of rayon 40 thread tend to unravel and create havoc in the work basket. A simple solution is to secure them with crossed-over rubber bands.

Requirements for lace and fabric dyeing.

Note: If swallowed, potassium permanganate is poisonous so please take care and keep out of reach of children.

ANTIQUE DYEING OF LACE USING POTASSIUM PERMANGANATE

There are many ways to age lace and fabric, but the one I prefer uses potassium permanganate which is a chemical in crystal form that can be purchased from most pharmacies in Australia and veterinary suppliers in the USA.

Today potassium permanganate is used as an anti-fungal agent in the treatment of animals but in the past it was used extensively for humans. When the crystals are added to water it turns a deep violet color but when oxidization occurs, the color changes to a wonderful golden brown.

When fabrics, laces or trims are treated with this mixture, the results, which are permanent, vary greatly according to the fabric type. This technique has many possibilities for the creative person and presents thrilling results.

MATERIALS
- *1 bottle of potassium permanganate crystals*
- *4 small plastic containers with lids*
- *1 small square paint brush*
- *1 pair of disposable gloves*
- *1 small plastic teaspoon*

TIP   Test all materials that are to be dyed as immersion time and concentration of the solution will determine the results. Fabric type is also a variant factor. The hotter the dye solution, the faster the dye takes. Remember to let the lace dry completely in order to see the finished color. It will be several shades lighter than the wet dyed lace.

1 Cover a flat surface with several layers of paper towel or scrap fabric and put on the plastic gloves. Completely fill three of the plastic containers with hot water

2 Place a quarter of a teaspoon of potassium

1. Wet lace goes into
weaker dye mix.

2. Accenting with
stronger dye.

3. Lace is paler
when dry.

permanganate crystals in one container of hot water and mix thoroughly. One-third fill the fourth container with boiling water then add a quarter of a teaspoon of potassium permanganate crystals and mix thoroughly until all the crystals are dissolved.

3 Immerse the lace in the clean water and then the weaker mixture of dye.

4 Lay the lace flat, then use the stronger solution of dye and the paintbrush to accent sections of the lace. Leave dye on the lace for 30-50 seconds (this time determines the strength of color).

5 Rinse the lace in clean water and lay flat to dry.

6 Dry the lace with heat, either the sun or an iron, to speed up the oxidization process.

This dye is permanent and will not wash out. Silk and rayon fibers produce particularly appealing colors when dyed this way and when combined with other materials give interesting results.

HAND PAINTED LACE

Hand colored laces added charm and beauty to many Victorian projects. Using Dylon or Rit dyes

from a pharmacy or supermarket a similar effect can be achieved with relative ease.

✂ TIP ✂ To 'age' the dyes, add a little black or brown to the mixed dye to soften the colors.

MATERIALS

✎ Dylon/Rit cold water dyes to suit (three colors)
✎ 4 small containers with lids
✎ 3 square paint brushes
✎ 4-5 sheets of paper towel

Note: Rayon laces give the best results when using this technique. Always test dye and let the lace dry before you embark on a major project as the colors change when completely dry.

1 Mix the dyes with cold water in separate containers according to the amount of dyeing and strength of color desired. Add aging colors, either black or brown, to mixed dye.

2 Immerse the lace piece in clean water, then lay it on a flat surface.

3 Use the paintbrush to paint the first color on to the wet lace in the areas of your choice.

4 Paint second color to unpainted areas of the lace

1. Paint color onto
wet lace.

2. Allow second color
to 'bleed' into first.

3. Highlight with a third
deeper neutral.

4. True color is revealed
when dry.

allowing the colors to 'bleed' into one another.

5 Highlight areas of the painted lace with a third deeper neutral color.

6 Allow dye to take following manufacturers instructions (time determines the strength of color) before rinsing in cold water.

7 Lay flat to dry. The true color will be several shades lighter and is only seen when the lace is completely dry.

✂ TIP ✂ These dyes can be sealed and stored in the refrigerator to be re-used. Make sure all containers are clearly labeled.

APPLYING VLIESOFIX/WONDERUNDER TO THE BACK OF LACE

If the above products appear in the materials lists of any projects in this book, always proceed as per the instructions given below.

There are three ways of applying lace to fabric:
— sewing by hand or machine around the lace edge with either a matching or monofilament thread using a freehand technique
— gluing in place using a strong glue such as 450 which is suitable for craft projects that are not going to be washed
— ironing to the fabric using a double-sided fusible web (Vliesofix/Wonderunder).

The first two methods are self-explanatory and the third is explained here in easy steps.

1 Place a piece of paper on the ironing board. Place lace pieces wrong side up on top of paper.

2 Cut a piece of Vliesofix/Wonderunder the same size as the paper and place over the lace, rough side facing down, paper side up,.

3 Use steam and heat, to iron the Vliesofix/

Wonderunder to the back of the lace ensuring that the excess web is ironed to the paper.

4 Allow to cool before removing the paper side of the web. The lace will now be covered with a fine web and the excess will adhere to the paper.

5 Remove the lace from the paper, then pull away any excess web from around the edge of the lace. The small amounts of web trapped in the holes of the lace can either be pulled away by hand or will melt away when next ironed.

✂ TIP ✂ Fusible web is a heat and steam-dissolving bonding agent, so use plenty of steam. If your iron does not generate enough steam, then lightly mist the lace with water before applying heat,. To prevent the web sticking to the iron, use an appliqué mat.

BACKING PRINTS AND FABRIC WITH VLIESOFIX/ WONDERUNDER AND PELLON H640

Vliesofix/Wonderunder (fusible web)and Pellon H640 (fusible batting) bond to fabrics when steam and heat activate the bonding agent.

Place the print/fabric, right side up, over a same size piece of either the fusible batting (bonding side up) or double sided fusible web (rough side up) and apply steam iron. Peel away backing paper of fusible web before steam ironing it to fabric

The right side of prints can be steam ironed, but if you are a little nervous, use an appliqué mat over or under the print.

Note: Never iron the right side of the print directly onto the ironing board as fluff or lint may stick to the print. Use either an appliqué mat or a clean lint free piece of cotton cloth over the ironing board.

1. Lace wrong side up on piece of paper.

2. Iron Vliesofix/Wonderunder to lace, rough side down.

3. When cool, remove paper.

MACHINE EMBROIDERY

The machine embroidery in this book uses rayon 40 or metallic embroidery threads through the needle and pre-wound bobbins. All machine embroidery needs to be stabilized either from behind or with a liquid stabilizer. I use photocopy paper behind built-in stitch machine embroidery and self-adhesive tear-away for hooped embroidery. Where specific stabilizers are required they will be listed in the materials list. Built-in stitches, motif embroidery designs and PC-design software that interfaces with a domestic sewing machine, give the novice the same skills as the experienced sewer allowing the machinist to achieve expert results at the touch of a button.

The following explanations will help in categorizing machine embroidery techniques:

—appliqué – applying one piece of material to another and securing and sealing the edges with machine embroidery stitching

—freehand embroidery – achieving a free-wheeling type of stitching by lowering the feed dogs, using a freehand embroidery foot and guiding the fabric by hand rather than the feed dogs advancing the fabric through the machine

—freehand quilting, stipple quilting – quilting through several layers of fabric often in small, meandering and continuous figure eight shapes or following stenciled design lines using the above technique

—built-in stitches – with an amazing array of built-in machine stitches it is possible to create ribbons, braids, laces, heirloom and quilting effects by simply keeping the fabric going in the desired direction

—motif embroidery – created with an embroidery machine capable of using memory cards and a hoop to embroider elaborate embroidery designs with speed and accuracy

—design software embroidery – machine embroidery designs can be either created using the software or imported into the software from a floppy disk, then down loaded to a blank design card to be stitched out as above.

—three-dimensional embroidery – can be achieved

Top: Decorative cushion cover by Anna Siler with 3-D machine embroidered pansies from my disk. Right:Machine embroidered pansies from my pansy disk adorn the bodice and ties of an evening dress. The ties also feature my silk organza pansy prints.

using any of the above techniques so the embroidery can hold together when cut out to be applied to another surface or embroidery.

The above techniques can be used individually or collectively to achieve the most amazing effects of the highest quality with ease and accuracy.

FABRIC STABILIZER

All motif embroidery uses the self-adhesive stabilizer technique shown below, unless otherwise stated.

All fabrics used in machine embroidery need to be stabilized and there are many products on the market that make this easy.

With the introduction of hooped automatic machine embroidery a diversification of products, geared to make fabric stabilization easier, has come onto the market.

The one I use the most is a self-adhesive tear-away that does as the name implies; sticks to the back of the fabric and tears away with ease when the embroidery is complete.

When the self-adhesive tear-away is used in a hoop, the process of placement and hooping fabric is done away with as perfect placement is achieve with ease.

1 Place the hoop over the self-adhesive tear-away to use as a guide to cut out a piece that is 2.5cm (1in) larger on all sides than the inner hoop.

2 Hoop the self-adhesive tear-away as if it were fabric with the protective backing facing up. Ensure it is securely in the hoop and very tight and smooth.

3 Perforate the protective backing by running a pin around the inside of the hoop and remove the backing. The sticky side of the tear-away is now facing up.

4 Place the hooped tear-away in the machine ready for embroidery then choose and position the design you wish to sew on the screen of the sewing machine.

5 Place the fabric to be embroidered exactly in the position that the embroidery is to be sewn under the foot and needle, then press the fabric flat and smooth to the self-adhesive tear-away.

6 Embroider the design. Then remove the hoop from the sewing machine and carefully remove the fabric from the self-adhesive tear-away without taking the stabilizer out of the hoop. A hole in the shape of the embroidered motif will then appear in the center of the tear-away.

7 Simply cut a piece of self-adhesive tear-away large enough to amply cover the hole left from the embroidery and patch from the underside of the stabilizer so the sticky side is up, thus filling the hole. This process can be repeated as many times, as you like, until the adhesive has lost its grip.

✂ TIP ✂ The self-adhesive tear-way can easily be removed from the back of the embroidery using a pair of tweezers, or comes away with washing. Remember do not iron the embroidery until you have removed tear-away or removal is very difficult.

FEET, NEEDLES AND THREAD

Each project gives clear directions about which feet, needles and threads to use for machine and hand embroidery but here are some general rules.

1 Machine embroidery is best achieved using a size 80/90 large eyed needle which prevents the threads from shredding.

2 For hand embroidery with thread use a crewel needle in a size that suits your thread. For ribbon embroidery use a tapestry needle, again in a size to suit the ribbon. Beading should be done with a fine beading needle to ensure that the needle will fit through every bead, (beading thread which is strong

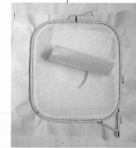

| 1. Calculating dimensions of tear-away. | 2. Hoop the tear-away, backing side up. | 3. Removing protective covering. | 4. Positioning fabric on adhesive surface. | 5. Patch hole from the underside of hoop. |

and doesn't stretch is also recommended, though in some cases I used monofilament thread)

3 Bobbin thread should be fine and strong, around a 70 or 80 denier and if your machine allows it, a pre-wound bobbin is time and cost efficient.

4 Machine embroidery threads are usually rayon 40 denier to achieve the best results.

5 Hand embroidery threads can be used in multiple or single strands for a fine or coarser finish.

6 Machine feet should suit the technique being used:

—an embroidery foot to suit your machine is used for motif embroidery

—clear-view freehand embroidery foot for freehand quilting and free-motion stitching

—open-toe embroidery foot for guided built-in stitches, to ensure accuracy when stitching

—five groove cording foot and blade for pin tucks

—narrow edge foot for stitching in-the-ditch

—zipper foot for stitching piping or top stitching

—dual-feed or walking foot for quilting and piecing.

QUILTING THROUGH WITH AUDREY'S BOND POWDER

A wonderful way to avoid pinning through all layers of a quilt and to prevent puckering during the final stages of assembly is to quilt through with Audrey's Bonding Powder.

1 When the quilt is pieced, cut the quilt backing up to 5cm (2in) larger on all four sides than the actual quilt.

2 Before applying the quilt backing, place quilt front right side down on the ironing board, batting facing up.

3 Lightly sprinkle Audrey's Bond Powder onto the batting, place quilt backing over batting making sure you center it and press in place with a hot iron. Work your way down the quilt ensuring the fabric is square and even. The bonding powder lightly fuses the quilt backing to the batting so that you can quilt though with ease, eliminating the need to pin. Should the fabric move, a light press with a steam iron will re-bond it.

1. Embroidery foot

2. Clear-view freehand embroidery foot

3. Open-toe embroidery foot

4. Five groove cording foot

5. Narrow edge foot

6. Zipper foot

7. Dual-feed walking foot

MITERING CORNERS

Mitering corners is joining fabric at a 45 degree angle to form a square edge (90 degree angle). It can be daunting, but need not be. There is a simple way to succeed every time with ease and confidence and the following steps will guide you. The photos refer to lace, but the same technique can be used in fabrics for cushions, tablecloths and patchwork.

1 When planning a mitered corner lay the lace/fabric on a flat surface, right side up, to create the desired corner, overlapping the strips to be mitered by the width of the strips of fabric/lace being joined. The top strip is A and the bottom strip is B.

2 If you are attaching this to another piece of fabric/lace then pin this to the edge of the fabric, allowing for the overlap to miter the corner. Stitch the fabric/lace to the edge of the fabric starting and finishing 6mm (1/4in) on either side of the corner.

3 Fold the end of strip A back and under until the end of the A fabric/lace strip is aligned with the underside edge of strip A and over strip B.

4 Press and pin the fold line.

5 Turn to the wrong side of the fabric/lace strip and pin along the fold line with right sides of strips together.

6 To check that the angle is correct, if you are joining fabric/lace to another fabric, fold the 90 degree of the corner (of the fabric that is being joined onto) in half to form a 45 degree angle. The pin line and subsequent seam line should be an extension of the fold line, thus forming a straight line. Sew a seam along the pinned line from corner to corner.

7 From the wrong side, trim the excess fabric from strips A and B to a 6mm (^{1}/4in)-seam allowance for fabric and as small as possible for lace then press the seam open.

8 If working with lace, turn to the right side of the lace and sew over the seam with a small zigzag stitch to secure the raw edges of the lace on the wrong side.

1. Determining fold line of lace.

2. Pin along lace fold line on wrong side.

3. Check fold line aligns with half-corner fold of fabric.

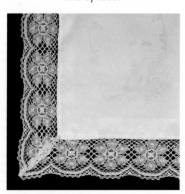

4. On wrong side, trim miter seam after stitching.

5. From right side, zigzag over miter seam to secure lace.

QUILT BINDING

Cut the quilt binding fabric either on the straight or bias, according to your preference.

As the binding is folded in half lengthwise before it is stitched, allow a generous width, say around 10cm (4in).

Bias Binding

1 Cut the fabric on the bias. A good method of doing this is to fold a fabric square into a double thickness triangle. Bias is on the long side. Fold this long side in half. With rotary cutter on mat, cut into four-thickness strips. Remember to allow for 6mm ($1/4$in) seams and the center lengthwise fold.

2 Join the bias pieces in one continuous strip, always joining them on the straight grain of the fabric to avoid a bubbled seam (the join will be at a 45-degree angle to the edge of the strip.)

3 Iron this strip in half lengthwise, with the wrong sides and the raw edges together.

4 Cut strips of Vliesofix/Wonderunder no more than 2.5cm (1in) wide. Iron this (paper side uppermost) to the edge of the bias strip so that it sits exactly on the folded edge; this will now be the wrong side of the quilt binding. Do not peel the paper from the back of Vliesofix/Wonderunder as the sticky surface revealed tends to be a nuisance when you machine stitch.

5 Round the corners of the quilt then pin the binding, with wrong side of the binding facing up and the raw fabric edges of the binding and quilt aligned, to the right side of the quilt. Attach the binding to the quilt with a straight stitch, using an open-toed foot with the dual feed attached (or a walking foot) allowing a 6mm ($1/4$in) seam allowance.

6 Join the binding by turning under the raw edges of one end of the bias strip and slipping the other end, into the fold; seam through all layers.

7 Peel the paper from the back of the Vliesofix/Wonderunder and fold the binding over to the wrong side of the quilt so the folded edge (with the Vliesofix/Wonderunder residue beneath it) just covers the row of stitching just completed. Iron in place using a hot steam iron, working on all four straight sides first and leaving the corners to last.

8 Ease the curve with your fingers just prior to

1. Cutting bias strips with rotary cutter.

2. Joining strips on straight grain of fabric.

3. Folding in half lengthwise, wrong sides together.

4. Ironing fusible web strip to folded edge of fabric.

5. Stitching to quilt edge, paper still on web strip.

6. Ironing binding in place, do corners last.

pressing with the iron. This will hold permanently without stitching. You may choose to stitch-in-the-ditch from the right side with transparent thread to add extra strength to the binding.

Straight Binding
Straight binding is attached in four separate pieces; two opposite sides first then the top and bottom.
1 Cut the fabric on the straight to suit your needs following the bias technique and join if necessary. You will need at least 7.5cm (3in) longer than each side.
2 Treat with Vliesofix/Wonderunder as above and attach the binding to either side of the quilt as above and remove the backing paper from the Vliesofix/Wonderunder. Fold binding to the back of the quilt and iron as before then trim the binding ends level with the quilt.
3 Work from the right side of the quilt centering the top and bottom binding strips over the quilt, with the raw edges of the binding aligned with the raw edges of the quilt. Fold the 3.5cm (1^1/2in) overhangs to the back of the quilt and pin before attaching the binding as before, stitching though all

layers of fabric.
4 Fold the binding up, then iron a small piece of Vliesofix/Wonderunder to the underside fabric of the fold and peel away the backing paper.
5 Fold over the binding strips and press in place as before. You may choose to stitch-in-the-ditch as before to finish the binding but is not necessary.

PAINTING PANSIES
All my pansy fabric prints started out as fabric paintings that I further embellished with embroidery and lace. After they proved to be popular in my classes, I had them printed on a variety of fabrics such as silk organza, silk dupion, delustered satin and moiré grosgrain. If you want to experiment with painting pansies, start on paper first to perfect your technique. Beginners often appreciate a bit of help at the start so trace over the basic shapes and follow the sequence and brush strokes to achieve a lifelike representation of a pansy. When you are confident enough to paint on fabric, keep the fabric taut and stable by stretching it over a piece of cardboard and securing it with adhesive tape.

FOLDED RIBBON ROSES

1 Fold the raw edge down a little them roll the ribbon three or four times to form the center of the rose. Secure with a few stitches. See pic 1.

2 Fold the ribbon on the cross; each fold becomes a petal. See pic 2.

3 Pull the center of the rose down when you roll the ribbon around it so the top of the fold is level with the center. Stitch the base of the rose after each fold.

4 Keep folding and stitching until you have the size and shape you want. A few folds will make a bud. Lots will make a full blown rose. See pic 3.

1   2   3

HAND EMBROIDERY STITCHES

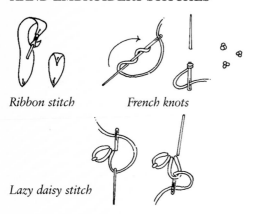

Ribbon stitch   French knots

Lazy daisy stitch

WIRED RIBBON PANSIES
MATERIALS

❧ For the petals: 25mm (1in) wide wire edged ribbon in two shades of one color

❧ For cutting: two pairs of scissors – one reserved specifically for cutting through wire edged ribbon

❧ For sewing: long darning needles, heavy non-slippery thread to match wire edged ribbon such as top stitching thread or buttonhole twist

❧ For stabilizing: lightweight buckram

❧ For the center: 25mm (1in) wide unwired ribbon in chartreuse or lemon, a pair of flat ended tweezers (optional) for making pinch pleats prior to knotting the center.

Note: The increment for measuring ribbon when making wired ribbon flowers is the width of the ribbon (referred to as WR in the following instructions). All the lengths that are cut are multiples of the width. For accurate measuring in order to ensure that the petals achieve life-like fullness, mark out the exact width of your ribbon between two pins, and use this gauge to measure lengths before cutting.

Method

Two upper petals or 'ears':

Cut two 4WR lengths of darker wire edged ribbon. Overlap to make a right angle. Knot thread and oversew at edge 3mm (1/8in) from start. Using 6mm (1/4in) long stitches, follow stitching lines in photograph. When the stitching travels diagonally to the other side, plot its arrival point by measuring a ribbon width from the starting edge. Draw in thread (not too tightly) and with tails pointing down, anchor with tacking stitches in the 'ditches' of folds to a piece of lightweight buckram.

Three lower petals or 'cheeks' and 'beard':

Cut one 12 WR length. Divide it in thirds and fold as in photograph, pinning diagonal corners for stability. Knot thread and oversew at edge 3 mm (1/8in) from start. Using 6mm (1/4in) long stitches, follow stitching lines in photograph. Tug firmly on thread to make a small center, backstitch to secure and knot. Do not cut thread. Bring the beginning and ending knots together stitching through the beginning knot and tug to close the gap. Hold the petals together and backstitch and knot again before cutting the thread. A tiny hole is left in the middle.

The center:

Loosely knot the center ribbon over the nail of the middle finger of the secondary hand (left if your are right-handed) with the ties hanging down. With tweezers or fingernails of the other hand, make tiny pleats across the 'flat' of the knot and hold firmly when you pull on the ties. Then thread the ties through the hole left in the 'beard' and 'cheek' petals, trim ties and stitch center and lower petals in place below the 'ears' on the buckram. Trim away excess buckram.

Note 1: Use thread to match color of wire edged ribbon. Contrasting thread is used in the photograph for the sake clarity.

Note 2:Instead of knotted 25mm (1in) wide ribbon for center, thread a chenille needle with

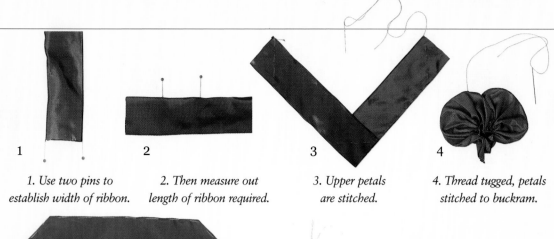

1. Use two pins to
establish width of ribbon.

2. Then measure out
length of ribbon required.

3. Upper petals
are stitched.

4. Thread tugged, petals
stitched to buckram.

5. Lower petals are
stitched.

6. Lower petals tugged
and knotted.

7. Start and finish of lower
petals stitched together.

8. Finished pansy with
center knotted ribbon.

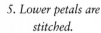

very narrow ribbon and work three French knots
into the pansy center, remembering to wrap the
ribbon twice around the needle more loosely
than you would if using embroidery thread. Yet
another method is to bead the center with tiny
beads in colors that contrast with the petals.

SCRUNCHED WIRED RIBBON LEAVES

1 This leaf has more gathers on one side than the
other so the leaf curves more in one direction.

2 Cut a 10$\frac{1}{2}$ RW length. Place horizontally before
you and fold to the back at 3$\frac{1}{2}$ RW from left. Turn
up lower left folded corner to make a 45-degree
angle and pin.

3 Along the lower side of the front ribbon section
where fold occurs, pull wire to gather to fit short
ribbon at back keeping one RW adjacent to the
pulled wire smooth. Then turn up this corner - the
piece is now a boat shape.

4 Turn 'boat' upside down and stitch by hand very
close to the edge along folded angled edge, the
shorter of the parallel sides of the ribbon boat and
then along the other folded angled edge.

5 Turn and glue or hand stitch in place with seam
against the right side of the fabric/print/embroidery.

PANSY RIBBON EMBROIDERERY BY MACHINE

The exquisite cushion on page 10 created by Cindy
Losekamp is an amazing example of ribbon
embroidery, done by machine, that would fool even
the most ardent hand embroiderer.

The sampler cushion is based on designs from the
Pfaff Martha Pullen embroidery card No 41. The
leaf section only of each design is stitched, then the
flowers are created using the ribbon embroidery by
machine technique to perfectly emulate hand
embroidery.

The pansy motif, which is of special interest to me,
is a looped ribbon flower made up of five petals
using 7mm wide silk ribbon.

The instructions are given for the pansy block only,
which could be used as the center of a small
cushion, or repeated for a larger one. Should you
wish to make the complete cushion please see the
credits on page 95.

Technique

The cushion is made from black silk dupion backed
with Pellon H640 (fusible batting). The machine
embroidery is done using the self-adhesive tear-away
technique on page 86 as a stabilizer in the hoop.

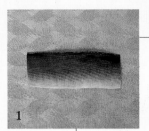 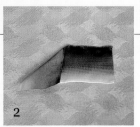 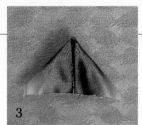 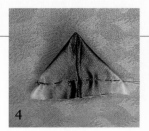 

1 2 3 4 5

Leaves with thread

The Pellon backed silk is adhered to the self-adhesive tear-away for the machine embroidery. Select design No 7, green rayon 40 embroidery thread, a pre-wound bobbin and a size-80 embroidery needle to stitch the leaves manually advancing through the flowers using the number 8 key.

Pansies with ribbon

Place monofilament thread in the bobbin, winding at half speed and only three-quarter filling the bobbin. Lower the feed dogs and thread a size-60 needle with monofilament thread. You do not use a foot but must engage the tension. Hoop the fabric with a spring tension hoop.

✂TIP✂ Always anchor threads by taking one stitch, drawing up the bobbin thread through the fabric and sew a few stitches up and back. Clip excess threads. The pansies are made from 7mm ribbon, one card of each in the following colors: light lilac, amethyst, deep purple, medium yellow and ivory silk ribbon. The centers are made with 4mm ribbon in deep yellow with the little loop details in very dark purple 4mm ribbon. White glass beads are used for buds, and tweezers (serger tweezers work well) are used for manipulating the ribbon.

Work with a continual length of ribbon, clipping as you go. The pansies are stitched in place of the omitted floral embroidery.

1. Anchor the pleated (pinched with the tweezers) 7mm ribbon in the center of the pansy with several stitches then make a 7mm (3/8 in) loop over the top, then pinch stitch the looped ribbon over the previous stitching. Repeat for all petals.

2. You will need to make five of these for each flower. Use two colors for each flower, with two loops of one color and three of another.

3. Secure the deep purple 4mm ribbon in the center of the ribbon pansy petals then make three small

---

WIRED RIBBON LEAVES

1. Remove wire from one side of ribbon. Cut piece to measure 2 RW in length.
2. Establish the center of the ribbon length and fold down at the point from the wired side.
3. Fold the other side down.
4. Hand stitch along the bottom.
5. Pull up and wind thread around leaf bottom and stitch through to secure. (Photo shows right side of leaf.)

---

loops, stitching each in place then tie off and clip excess ribbon and threads.

4. Attach the 4mm deep yellow ribbon in the center of the petals and whiskers then make a French knot with this ribbon to form the center of the pansy:
— anchor the tip of the ribbon in the center of pansy
— sink the needle tip into the fabric.
— wrap the ribbon around the needle 3 times
— hand wind the fly wheel for one stitch. When the needle is out of the fabric, lay knot down and bring leftover ribbon around to the center. Stitch and trim off excess.

5. Create buds using glass beads, this is done at the end, so do so when you have completed all the embroidery.

Machine beading:
— anchor thread at the base of bead placement, trim tails
— do not use needle down, to avoid breaking needles and pearls
— hand wheel the needle so it is at the point of piercing the fabric.
— place one bead on the tip of the needle
— with the bead on the needle, drag the needle tip the width of the bead, past the placement position
— hand wheel the needle to make a stitch
— after the first stitch, drag the needle back to the starting point.

This action causes the bead to roll over and hide the hole and thread. Don't be surprised if you break a few needles when you first start. This is normal and breakage diminishes after a little practice. Continue stitching on the beads, traveling between each one with a small running stitch. There is no need to break your threads after each bead. If you should break your needle, don't panic. Just replace the needle, tie off your threads and begin again.

Suppliers

U.S.A.

Pfaff American Sales Corp
610 Winters Avenue
Paramus New Jersey
07653 0566
Phone: 201 262 7221
Fax: 201 262 0696

Pollard's Sew Creative
(US distributor of Jenny Haskins products)
1934 E. Alosta Avenue
Glendora, CA 91740
Phone: 626 335 2770
Fax: 626 335 4960
Email: victoriaann@earthlink.net
Web site: http://www.pollardsew-creative.com

Quality Sew & Vac
AAA Store
10859 1st Ave. S
Seattle, Wash. 98072
Phone: 206 244 5555

Everett Store
10121 Evergreen Way
Everett, WA 98204
Phone: 800 488 0458

Associated Sewing
690 Snelling Ave
St Paul MN 55104

Bakers Sewing Center
112 N Kalmia St
Escondido CA 92025
Phone: 760 745 4140

Beaches Sew & Vac
Center
6600 Dixie Hwy
Fairfield OH 45014
Phone: 513 874 4900

Charlotte's Sewing
Center
11048 Manchester Rd
St Louis MO 63122
314 965 3848

Dry Creek Quilts
6470 W 120th Ave
Broomfield CO 80020
Phone: 303 465 2526

English Sewing
Machine
7001 Benton Rd
Paducah
Kentucky 42003
Phone: 502 898 7301

Ericas Craft & Sew
Center
1320 N Ironwood Dr
South Bend
IND 46615
Phone: 219 233 3120

Fit To Sew
7217 S Western Ave
Oklahoma City
OK 73139
Phone: 405 631 2663

Flights Of Fancy
4005 Mesa Ridge
Fortworth TX 76137
Phone: 800 530 8745

Hearts All Around
2614 Kiddy Rd
Jackson MI 49203
Phone: 517 789 8228

McKee's Sewing
Center
2516 E 15th St
Tulsa OK 74104
Phone: 918 744 5403

Peg & Lil's Needle
Patch
127 Peddlers Way
Washington IL 61571
Phone: 309 444 7667

Place That Sells Sewing
Machines
1462 Mendocino Ave
Santa Rosa CA 95401
Phone: 707 575 5259

Rays Vac & Sewing
Center
985 Asheville Hwy
Spartanburg SC 29303

Satin Stitches Sewing
& Emb.
705 D Vaniver Dr
Columbia MD 65202
Phone: 573 817 0006

Sharmans Sewing
Center
1017 McCann Rd
Longview TX 75601
903 753 8014

Moores Sewing Center
25390 Marguerite Pl
Mission Viejo CA
92692

Threads Of Time
3125 Sheridan Dr
Amherst NY 14226

AUSTRALIA

Unique Creative
Opportunities
(for Jenny Haskins Victorian Prints, Disks and Antique Laces)
(wholesale and retail)
PO Box 2156
Carlingford Court
NSW 2118
Ph/fax: 02 9873 3655
Email: jenny@rpi.net.au
Web site: http://www.jennyhaskins.com

Anne's Glory Box
60 Beaumont Street
Hamilton NSW 2303
Phone: 02 4961 6016
Fax: 02 4961 6587
Web site: http://www.textiletraders.comau/agb.htm

Perth Sewing Centre
Unit 5/12-14 Baretta
Road
Wangarra WA 6065
Phone: 08 9309 5199
Fax: 08 9409 2094
Email: psc@netl.nw.com.au

Janome/Pfaff Sewing
Centre Parramatta
Shop 2172
Westfield Shopping
Centre
Parramatta NSW 2150
Phone: 02 9893 9954
Fax: 02 9687 9161

Hobbysew
2 Railway Street
Pennant Hills
NSW 2120
Phone 02 9980 8966
Fax 02 9980 9497

The Remnant Box
94 Nelson Street
Wallsend NSW 2287
Phone 02 4953 8400
Fax 02 4953 8401

Romantique
68 Milton Parade
Malvern VIC 3144
Phone 03 9822 52 93
Fax 03 9804 3665

Castle Hill Sewing
Centre
Shop1 No1, Castle
Street,
Castle Hill NSW 2154
Phone 02 9894 8994
Fax 02 9894 7676

Sew Together Pty
Limited
768 Hunter Street
Newcastle West
NSW 2302
Phone 02 4969 3189
Fax 02 4959 5011

World of Sewing
Shop 35 A-F Westfield
Shoppingtown
Hunter Street
Hornsby NSW 2077
Phone 02 9476 6142

Heirloom Studio
303 Dungog Road
Martins Creek
NSW 2420
Phone/Fax 02 4938
8134
Mobile phone: 0409
986565

Sewing Machine
Doctor
Shop 68 A Oatley
Court
Belconnan ACT 2617
Phone 02 6251 4349
Fax 02 6251 4349

Sew'n' Sew Quilters
Paradise
69 Juilette Street
Annerley QLD 4103
Phone 07 3891 6999
Fax 07 3891 6999

Ron Morgan Sewing
Machines
157 Adelaide Street
Maryborough
QLD 4650
Phone 07 4123 1011
Fax 07 4125 1594

Melann's Fabrics &
Sewing Centre
850 Lower North East
Road
Dernancourt SA 5075
Phone 08 8337 7548
Fax 08 8337 7548

All Make Sewing
Centre
330 Goodwood Road
Clarence Park SA 5034
Phone 08 8373 1226
Fax 08 8271 8644

Stewarts Sewing
Machine Centre
Cnr William & Best Sts
Devonport TAS 7310
Phone 03 624 5440
Fax 03 624 8838

Liz's Sewing Centre
Shop 17, Dorset
Square
Boronia VIC 3155
Phone 03 9762 6633
Fax 03 9762 6355

Camberwell Sewing
Centre
849 Burke Road,
Camberwell VIC 3124
Phone 03 9882 7673
Fax 03 9882 2713

Simply Fabrics
Shop 1/60 Church St
Lakes Entrance
VIC 3909
Phone 03 5155 3253
Fax 03 5155 3253

Port Sewing Centre
58 Adelaide Street
Fremantle WA 6160
Phone 08 9335 6113
Fax 08 9430 5093

Carol's Fashion Fabrics
18 Victoria Street
Midland WA 6056
Phone 61 8 9250 2722
Fax 61 8 9250 2721

South West Sewing
Centre
Shop 2, The
Boulevarde, Princep St
Bunbury WA 6230
Phone 61 8 9721 2462
Fax 61 8 9721 2089

CREDITS

Blouse on page 10 designed and made by Marcia Pollard. Contact Pollard's Sew Creative (see US suppliers) for notes.

Silk ribbon cushion on page 10 designed and made by: Cindy Losekamp c/- Beaches Sew & Vac Center (see US suppliers). Notes for the cushion can be obtained if you email: CLosekamp@aol.com

Pansy Sewing Case on page 27 and Four Beauties on a Fan Quilt on page 48 designed and made by Lucienne Magnay of Unique Creative Opportunities (see Aus. suppliers).

Heart of a Pansy, page 36, Cluster of Cushions, page 38, Framed Pansy Basket, page 62 and Pansy Boudoir Hanger, page 76 designed and made by Gloria McKinnon of Anne's Glory Box (see Australian suppliers).

Lady in Waiting quilt on page 72 designed and made by Sheila Pye of Perth Sewing Centre (see Aus suppliers).

Pansies in a Vase, page 85 designed and made by Anna Siler of Janome/Pfaff Sewing Centre Parramatta, (see Australian suppliers).

Pansy Evening Dress, pages 85 & 87 is Vintage Vogue pattern No 2239.

—— ❖ ——

14,710 Dirty Diapers

2,576 Loads of Laundry

33 Skinned Knees

228 Soccer Games

4,761 Hours of Homework

108 Check-ups

97 Bake Sales

3 Proms

4 Graduation Ceremonies

—— ❖ ——